For Richer, Not Poorer

For
RICHER,
Not
POORER

The Money Book
for Couples

Ruth L. Hayden

Health Communications, Inc.
Deerfield Beach, Florida

www.hci-online.com

Library of Congress Cataloging-in-Publication Data

Hayden, Ruth L., date.
    For Richer, not poorer : the money book for couples / Ruth L.
Hayden.
        p.   cm.
    Includes index.
    ISBN 1-55874-718-4 (trade paper)
    1. Married people—Finance, Personal.   2. Finance, Personal.
I. Title.
HG179.H345   1999
332.024'0655—dc21   99-37493
                                                                            CIP

Publisher: Health Communications, Inc.
                3201 S.W. 15th Street
                Deerfield Beach, Florida 33442-8190

Cover design by Larissa C. Hise
Book design by Lawna Patterson Oldfield

To Don
My partner and friend
for thirty years
and counting

Contents

Acknowledgments

I would like to acknowledge all the couples that allowed me to help them create a partnership in their money lives. The changes these couples created in their lives inspired me to write *For Richer, Not Poorer*.

Thank you to all the wonderful professionals at Health Communications, including Peter Vegso, Teri Peluso, Matthew Diener, Lisa Drucker and Christine Belleris. The respect you showed me while producing my first book, *How to Turn Your Money Life Around: The Money Book for Women*, has been more than duplicated while working on this book. Thank you.

Thank you to Diane Beyer, Elizabeth Quam Berne and Martha Malan for all your encouragement and support. Thanks to Laura Beaudoin for her excellent editing, and to Greg and Sally Rademacher at Rademacher's Studio for the photograph.

And finally, I would like to thank my children. Jennifer, Steven, Nathan and Christina, like all children, have provided wonderful motivation for making Don's and my partnership work long-term. You kids are great!

How This Book Can Help You

T he couples that come to my office have few outward similarities. They are individuals of various ages, physical shapes and social and economic backgrounds. Some of the couples have been together for decades, and others are newly together. They come with varying degrees of commitment to their relationship and to the money work we will be doing. And yet they all come because the process of financial change they learn in my office works. It's that simple. The process works.

For Richer, Not Poorer teaches you this same process. Just like the couples that come to my office, you may have varying degrees of commitment to each other and to the money work you will be doing. You, like them, may feud, fight, cry and laugh as you learn. Still, the process you learn in this book will change your money life.

In this book, you will:

- name the four cornerstones of a healthy money partnership;

- recognize the methods of communicating as a couple that do not create a long-term financial partnership—and the methods that do;
- uncover your beliefs about money, which control your behaviors with money;
- identify your mutual values and goals, which form the foundation of your budget planning;
- describe the two absolute rules of budgeting;
- learn a step-by-step process for developing a workable budget that you both are committed to—emotionally and intellectually.

For Richer, Not Poorer teaches you an evolutionary process to make your money life work in a way that helps you form a strong, committed, lifetime partnership. This book is *not* a quick fix, and it doesn't tell you what kind of investments to make. This book is about cash flow. It is about learning to work together as a self-empowered team. The process outlined in this book will work for you for a lifetime. Even as your life changes and the numbers in your budget change, the methods, strategies and skills will continue to work.

If you were single, you could probably skip through this book and still learn the process. But you are not single. You are in a couple relationship, and you need a format for working together that you can both agree to follow. So, follow the process in the book, step by step, and it will work for both of you.

Each of you will need a notebook, a pen or pencil, and a timer. You also need a quiet place and time to work together and individually on the exercises. If you have children, this is difficult. I tell the couples that come to my office to get a baby-sitter and either stay home or get out of the house and go to a quiet place with no distractions. If you stay at home, turn off the phone and don't answer the door. Think of this time as an investment in your life together.

In addition to the actual budgeting part of your money life—adding, subtracting and making lists—you will also learn about the management part of money. This management part involves talking about your relationship, about your money beliefs and about your history. One of you may be more comfortable with this management part and the other more comfortable with the budgeting part. In this book, you will each learn how to feel comfortable with both parts. This is necessary if you are really going to learn a new, more effective way of working with money—together.

Step by step you will learn a new way to work together in your money life, just as thousands of other couples have learned.

One

Our Money Life Is *Not* Working

I can't take much more of this," David explains. "I really love Julie, and she's terrific—she's a good mother, we have a lot in common and I like her sense of humor. But, Ruth," he explodes, "she's going to drive us into bankruptcy!"

"That's not fair!" Julie interrupts angrily. "I had to buy Sara clothes because she's grown another two inches. Should I tell the children we have to skip birthdays this year? And, what about the two suits you just *had* to buy? The problem isn't *my* spending," she continues angrily. "The truth is that you just don't make enough money to support this family."

"But Julie, I've *never* earned enough according to you. Never! Why don't you—yes, *you*—get a job and help out a little instead of always complaining?"

Julie is totally exasperated. "I can't, David, you know that.

1

No job that I can get pays enough to cover child care. Remember? If I get a job, it'll have to be after the kids are all in school. So, leave me alone."

"Julie," David continues, "I've said it before and I'll say it again, you're just like your mother. You're going to drive me into bankruptcy just like she did to your father."

Now Julie is *really* angry. "That's not true and you know it! Why do you always have to be so mean and bring my parents into this?"

FACT: Money is the number-one reason for conflict in a relationship.

Many couples, like Julie and David, say that a primary cause of conflict in their relationships is money. Who should earn the money? How much is needed? Conflict also arises over decisions about what purchases to make and how much money to spend on each purchase.

Your Turn

[Directions: Please write your answers—individually—to the "Your Turn" exercises throughout the book.]

- Do you believe that conflict in a relationship can be caused by money?

- Can a discussion about how much money is enough cause conflict?

- Do you and your partner ever argue about the amount of money to spend on something? Describe the conflict.

- Do you and your partner ever argue over the amount of money you earn? If so, is the conflict over the *amount* of money or the *lack* of money earned? Is the conflict over the amount of time you spend away from home earning money?

- Do you identify with what David says or with what Julie says? What makes you identify with one or the other?

Maria and Jack

Maybe this conversation between Maria and her husband, Jack, is more familiar to you:

"Ruth, if Jack's new business doesn't start making money soon, I'm not going to make it." Maria cries as she continues, "I wake up in the middle of the night scared out of my wits, unable to breathe. My doctor says I'm having panic attacks. He says the way to stop them is to get rid of the stress in my life. Get rid of the stress! As long as Jack is spending money starting this business, I can't get rid of the stress."

Maria's voice rises. "Don't you understand, Ruth, I'm afraid we'll lose our house. Jack took out a second mortgage to start his business, and he's already three months behind in the payments. And, our credit cards are all at their limits. I'm working all the overtime I can get and it's still not enough." Her voice drops to a whisper, "I just don't want to lose my home."

"Maria," Jack explodes, "I can't concentrate on my business when I have to listen to how afraid you are all the time. You wake yourself up in the middle of the night and then wake me up as well. Come on, you're supposed to support me. You told me when I started that you would. I finally get to be my own boss and you want to stop me!"

"Now you're blaming me?" Maria asks with tears in her

eyes. "I work double shifts at the hospital to make more money. When I'm home, I do all the housework so you can work at the business. And I'm doing most of the parenting. I *am* keeping my commitment! You know I am!"

"The point is," Maria continues, "what about our house? How are you going to pay the overdue payments? What will happen to us if we lose our home?"

"I've told you before, Maria," Jack says angrily, enunciating each word slowly, "we're *not* going to lose the house. Come on, Maria, this is my dream. You've got to trust me on this."

"I don't know if I can, Jack," Maria says. "I just don't know if I can."

FACT: Money is the number-one reason for stress and anxiety in a relationship.

Couples like Jack and Maria have different comfort levels with the amount of debt they carry. Jack is much more comfortable with substantial debt than Maria. This is why taking on debt causes stress and conflict for many couples. Couples take on debt in many ways:

- by obtaining a larger mortgage on their home through refinancing;
- by taking out a second mortgage on their home;
- by increasing the amount they owe on credit cards;
- by getting a line of credit from the bank;
- by borrowing from the cash value of their life insurance;
- by borrowing from their 401(k) plan;
- by borrowing from parents or other relatives.

It's all debt. Any one of these debts has the potential to cre-ate anxiety. Any one of these debts can create conflict in your relationship.

Your Turn

- Do you believe people have different levels of comfort with debt?

- How would you describe your own level of comfort with debt? How much debt would make you uncomfortable?

- How much debt would cause you to feel anxiety?

- What kinds of debt would cause you the most anxiety? Why?

- Now, answer these same questions as if you were your partner.

- Is there any stress in your relationship due to your different comfort levels with debt?

- Are the fear and anxiety Maria expressed familiar to you? Explain.

- Is the frustration Jack expressed familiar to you? Explain.

Will and Diane

Will and Diane may sound more familiar to you:

"We'll never get ahead," Will begins as he and Diane sit in my office one afternoon. "I'm forty-four years old, and I don't see how I'll ever be able to retire. We're not in any big finan-cial crisis. We don't even fight about money. We're just so discouraged."

"You see," Diane says, "we have two children. They're both in high school, and they both want to go away to college. But how will we ever pay for it? We kept waiting to save until Will got a promotion, but he never did, so we haven't saved a thing. I just can't believe how fast the years have gone by."

"It isn't as if I haven't tried," Will says. "I put my paycheck in the bank each month and pay the bills, and each month I think there will be something left over to put away. But something always comes up. *Always*. I'm exhausted from trying."

"I always thought I'd have my college degree by now so I could help out," Diane continues. "I dropped out of college when I became pregnant with our daughter, and we haven't been able to afford the time and money for me to go back and finish. I'm so discouraged. I'm tired of constantly trying to figure out where the money went. And I'm tired of Will telling me it's my fault there's nothing left at the end of the month."

"I'm frustrated, too," Will adds. "I look in the mirror and I see *old*. There have been layoffs at my company. I worry all the time. What if *I* get laid off? What if I can't keep juggling the bills?"

> **FACT: Money is the number-one reason for frustration and discouragement in a relationship.**

Many couples, like Will and Diane, are frustrated that they can never get ahead. They have no real financial crisis, but the ongoing stress their discouragement causes wears them out individually and as a couple. And, underneath it all, conflict is building.

Your Turn

- Do you identify with Diane and Will? What specifically are you facing that is so discouraging? Maybe you thought by this time in your life you would:

    –be more successful;

    –have more money saved;

    –have your own business;

    –be more secure in your company position;

    –have finished your education;

    –be able to provide education for your children;

    –be able to travel;

    –have the home you really want;

    –have living room furniture that all matched;

    –be happier;

    –feel successful;

    –not feel so old.

- Why do you think your partner is discouraged?

- Are you experiencing stress in your relationship because of this discouragement? Are you experiencing conflict?

Larry and Kate

"I'm not really sure why we're here," Larry begins, "except that Kate wanted me to come and finally, with a bit of reticence, I agreed."

Larry's discomfort about being in my office is obvious. I nod for him to continue.

"I'm not really sure what Kate thinks is wrong about what we do with our money. After all, I'm a professional financial advisor. I know much more than she does about money."

Larry holds himself back from adding, "and probably more than you." I smile and ask him to continue.

"We split everything fifty-fifty. The bills are paid. We don't fight. Our kids are grown and on their own." This time Larry smiles as he finishes, "Well, sort of."

Kate interrupts by saying, "Why don't I explain why I wanted us to work with you, Ruth?" She leans forward as she continues. "Both Larry and I earn a good income. We have a nice life. Our children are finally settling into their lives. We have beautiful things and take nice trips. This *should* be the happiest and freest time of our lives, but it's not! Larry complains constantly about how stressful his job is, how little money we have put away for our ages—I'm fifty-three and Larry is fifty-eight. He complains that we spend too much, but what he really means is that *I* spend too much."

Kate looks at her husband, who's been quiet through all this, and says, "Larry wants to retire early, and I want that for him, too. His business really *is* stressful. But now he tells me he doesn't even think he'll be able to retire at sixty-five, because we haven't saved enough. He always says it in an accusatory way, and I don't know how to respond. So I just listen and stay silent. He wears out eventually, and we go on with our lives."

"But, Larry," says Kate, this time addressing him directly, "if what you say is true, then we need to make some changes. I just don't know what to do, and I'm tired of feeling accused."

I look at Larry and ask him if what Kate says accurately represents his concerns. Larry nods and then quietly says, "It seems almost too late to make much difference for the future."

Kate looks at him and says, "I don't believe it! You're just discouraged and mad."

> **FACT: Money is the number-one reason for anger and accusation in a relationship.**

Many couples, in the privacy of their own homes, communicate in an angry and accusatory way. Many times this anger comes from deep discouragement—which is what Larry is feeling. This discouragement may stem from a sense of shame. Larry is a successful financial advisor, but he hasn't been able to do for himself what he does for his clients. His shame is expressed as anger and accusation towards Kate. Neither Larry nor Kate knows what to do. Larry vents his discouragement, and Kate goes silent.

Your Turn

- Do you identify with Larry? If so, in what way?

- Can people become so discouraged that they, like Larry, sound mad and accusatory most of the time?

- Do you identify with Kate? Are you silent as your partner vents about money? If you are, what is this like for you?

- Can anger come from years and years of discouragement? Have you ever felt ongoing discouragement and expressed it as anger toward your partner? If so, what caused the discouragement? Is the discouragement still a part of your feelings today?

Anne and Neil

Maybe you identify more with Neil and Anne in this conversation:

"Ruth," Anne begins, "I want you to help me explain to Neil the importance of not wasting money. I am sick and tired of always having to be the responsible one and say, 'Now don't spend that' or 'Don't buy this because it's too expensive.' He's got to understand that we need to put more money in savings in case either of us decides to quit our job or we lose our jobs or in case something else happens."

Anne turns to her husband and says, "Neil, you've just got to stop spending so much money."

"Oh, come on, Anne, give me a break!" Neil shakes his head. "I earn plenty of money and you know it—more than we need. I work hard for every dime I make and I deserve to spend money on myself without you scolding me and telling me I can't. I'll tell you what, when you earn as much as I do, you can tell me when I can and can't spend!"

Neil looks at me. "Ruth, can't you explain to her that we're saving more than enough money for whatever catastrophes she keeps making up in her head? Can't you explain that a guy who works as hard as I do needs all the things I have because I need to relax and unwind—*and* because I've earned them?"

"All you want to do is have money to play," Anne says angrily. "You don't even care about what's important to me. You never listen to me and what I want. Never!"

"Here we go again," Neil interrupts. "Now she'll tell you that if I don't stop spending money, then I really don't love her. Right, Anne? I can't believe it. Round and round we go. . . ."

"Stop it, Neil. Just stop it!" Anne says angrily, "I'm through. I'm done trying to get you to be responsible. I quit. It's up to you, now. Since you earn the most income, it's up to you now. Just pay the basic house bills and I'll use my money to pay for my life. You figure it out—how much for toys and how much for retirement. Now are you happy?"

> **FACT: Money is the number-one reason for fussing and feuding in relationships.**

For many couples, like Neil and Anne, no matter how much or how little money they earn, money is the primary reason for fussing and feuding in their relationship. Money is the primary reason for couples fussing and feuding at the dinner table, on the couch and in the bedroom.

Whether fussing over the cost of recreational toys or feuding over retirement savings, these couples have conflict. Whether feuding over paying the mortgage or fussing about the cost of their children's clothing, they have conflict. Whether fussing over how much to spend on a vacation or feuding over the Visa bill, they have conflict.

Your Turn

- Is money the main reason couples fuss and feud and fight? Do you believe this is true no matter the income of the couple—whether they have a lot of money or little money?

- Do couples fuss and feud over big, expensive money decisions as much as they fuss and feud over small, daily expenses? Do you argue more over small items or large items? Why, do you suppose?

- What started the last money argument you and your partner had over a large money expenditure?

- What was the last argument you had over a small money expenditure?

- How do you think your partner would answer these questions?

Ted and Denise

Sometimes couples decide to stop all this fussing and feuding and quit fighting. Maybe Denise and Ted sound familiar to you:

"We've finally stopped fighting about money," Denise explains. "I think we've both just given up."

Ted nods as Denise continues. "Each month is more discouraging than the last. We used to be hopeful. We'd say, 'Next month, we'll have a little left over' or 'Next month we'll get ahead and maybe even go out for a nice dinner or something.' The next month would come, and we would still be behind."

"We had terrible fights," Ted confesses. "We'd call each other names and yell. We were both mean and nasty. We'd wear ourselves out and then not talk to each other for hours or even days. To me, this was a relief. Then, we would start talking again and everything would go back to normal."

"We would be divorced by now if we had continued to fight the way we did," Denise adds. "Even if it looked like things were back to normal, we had really hurt each other. It seemed that it took a little longer for us to come back together after each fight." With tears in her eyes, Denise says, "I know this sounds crazy, but I think we both gave up on the money in order to save our marriage."

"I agree," says Ted. "We couldn't keep hurting each other and stay married. But now, we feel hopeless. We're sending in bill payments late—if at all—and our Visa card is at its limit. We don't have any slack if we have an emergency. I hate those phone calls from people asking for their payments. Sometimes I don't even answer the phone. It's just plain discouraging. I keep working, but we'll never get ahead. We'll probably have to drive our old cars for another ten years, and I don't know how our kids will ever get to college. . . ."

"And," Denise interrupts, "we'll never get our honeymoon—ever. See, we couldn't afford a honeymoon when we got married because we were both in school. We promised ourselves we would take one someday, but I don't think that someday will ever come."

FACT: Money is the number-one reason for anxiety and hopelessness in a relationship.

Couples like Ted and Denise trade the fighting for greater anxiety over the money itself. Some couples believe they must stop talking about money in order to save their marriage. This doesn't work because they are not making decisions about money and are not in charge of their money life. Not only do couples like Denise and Ted live with the nearly constant anxiety of late payments and creditors calling, but they also live with a sense of hopelessness. They begin to believe that they will never get ahead and their money life will never change.

Your Turn

- Do Ted and Denise sound familiar to you?

- Have you decided to just stop fighting about money—really just stop? If so, why?

- What was happening in your relationship that made you decide to stop?

- What happened—good and bad—in your relationship when you stopped fighting about money? How did things change between you?

- When you stopped fighting about money, did the money tasks still get done—were the bills paid on time and the checkbook reconciled? Or did you fall behind in these tasks and let the money problems accumulate?

- How would your partner answer these questions?

Shelly and Rob

Shelly and Rob first asked for help several months after filing for personal bankruptcy. Shelly is a homemaker and Rob is a doctor in a small medical partnership. They are both in their late fifties.

Rob and his three medical partners had invested a fairly large amount of money based on financial advice that proved to be unsound. Rob had borrowed a great deal of money to cover his portion of the investment, in addition to taking out a second mortgage on their home. There was a lawsuit, and Rob lost a great deal of money, including a large portion of his retirement money. As a result, his projected retirement in four years was put on hold. They were able to keep their home but had to file personal bankruptcy.

When Shelly called me for an appointment, she said, "I don't ever want to go through this again. I feel completely powerless and I'm terrified. Rob has agreed to come because he knows how scared I am." I saw Shelly and Rob one time.

Almost two years later, Shelly has come in to see me—alone.

"My divorce from Rob has just been finalized," Shelly begins. "It was the only choice I had."

She continues, "Do you remember when you asked Rob two years ago if he would make an agreement with me, his wife, that the next time someone came to the office with some financial product to sell, he wouldn't make a decision until he had consulted with his accountant, his attorney and me? Remember, Ruth?"

I did remember this agreement.

"Rob said he couldn't make that agreement because he didn't want his partners to think he didn't know what he was doing and that he had to ask permission to make an investment. Well, that was my first warning. My second warning was that he refused to work on our money life as a couple. Ruth, we didn't come in to see you again because Rob said he wasn't about to be put on a budget. He told me, 'I'm a doctor and earn enough to have the freedom to spend the way I want to—and when I want to.'"

Shelly squares her shoulders and says, "As hard as the divorce has been and despite all the difficult things I will need to handle alone, I know that I feel saner and safer than I ever felt married to Rob. I have much less money, but I know where it is. I have a much smaller house now, but I know it's mine and I won't lose it. But I still feel sad over what we could have had together."

FACT: Money is the number-one reason couples separate or divorce.

When couples decide that they are tired of fighting, and they *also* decide they can't live with the hopelessness of never knowing if the money part of their lives will ever change for the better, then some decide to end their relationship, because they don't know any other way to live together.

Your Turn

- Do you ever wonder if you can continue to live like this? Do you ever wonder if you will have to end your relationship?

- How would your partner answer these questions?

Kim and Denny

If you both *are* still talking, perhaps you sound more like Kim and Denny:

"We're here on the advice of our marriage counselor," says Denny. "Our counselor suggested we give it one last try before splitting up. She suggested we see you since the only problem that really gets us is money. Oh, we argue about the kids, but that somehow works out."

"We argue about the in-laws," Kim interrupts, "but then we just live with it. And we argue about the time he spends with the guys and his bowling league, but somehow we get through it. But the money, Ruth . . ."

"Yeah, the money." Now it's Denny who interrupts. "She

spends money on the dumbest stuff."

"What about you?" asks Kim. "What about your bowling money and your lottery ticket money and your stopping-with-the-guys-after-work money?"

"Oh, come on, Kim," Denny protests. "That's nothing compared to your clothes money and your garage sale money."

"See, Ruth," Kim explains. "This goes on all the time. I can't do or spend anything without him criticizing me."

"Me, neither," interjects Denny. "All you do is criticize how I spend money. I'm ready to call it quits. A guy just can't live like this."

"I agree, Denny," Kim says softly. "I can't live like this either. I'm just so sick and tired of all this fighting about money. I don't even know exactly why we're here, Ruth. Maybe it's too late to help us."

Your Turn

- Ask yourself why you are reading this book.

- What experiences in your relationship motivated you to read this book?

- How do you think your partner answered this same question? Ask him or her to tell you. Then, tell your partner how you answered it.

- Which of the couples you read about in this chapter most expresses what you're thinking right now?

- What is happening in your money life—right now—to make you identify with the couple you chose? Be specific.

- Which couple do you think your partner most identifies with, and why? Ask him or her to tell you, and then tell your partner your answers.

Exercise: Taking Stock

In your individual notebooks, write "Chapter 1" at the top of the first page. Working alone and silently, answer the following questions. When you are finished writing, wait patiently and quietly until your partner is finished.

1. Is the spending and earning of money an area of conflict in your relationship? If so, what conflict are you experiencing right now?
2. Are you experiencing anxiety, stress, frustration or hopelessness in your relationship?
3. What do you think will happen to you and to your relationship if you and your partner don't find new ways to make decisions about money?
4. What do you think will happen to you and to your relationship if you and your partner don't stop fussing and feuding over money?

Exercise: Communicating with Your Partner

Take ten minutes each to read what you just wrote in your notebooks to your partner. Whoever is not reading should be the timekeeper. With this structure, each of you will talk for *no more* and *no less* than ten minutes. This structure is important, because it helps you balance the information the other gives you. One of you may not usually give the other much information about yourself, or one of you may typically give a great deal of information. If you adopt this structure, you will both know that this exercise will not turn into a "marathon" discussion, nor will one of you get away with sharing little or no personal information.

So, again, each of you has ten minutes—no more and no less. And don't interrupt.

Why We're Here

You picked up this book because you and your partner's money life isn't working so well, right? The way the two of you talk about money isn't working. The way you make money decisions together isn't working the way you would like it to work.

But wait a minute! What is even more important is that you both *want* your money life to work better. You are looking for new ways to work together and to talk about money. That's why you picked up this book. Allow yourself, maybe for the first time in a long time, to feel hope that you can change your money life if you are willing to work together.

Will you both—right now—make a commitment to continue working through this book? If your answer is yes, will you shake each other's hand as a symbol of your commitment? Come on! So you haven't shaken each other's hand in awhile. In our culture, a handshake symbolizes mutual respect when making an agreement. You are making an official agreement with each other—today.

So, take the time to shake hands and symbolize your commitment. All great change starts with small symbols. And the two of you are going to create great change in your money life as you work through this book.

Come on! Shake on it. Show each other you are committed to working through this book—committed to creating change.

Congratulations! Your commitment is a decision to change the way you work with your money. A decision is not a "maybe." A decision doesn't mean you will just see what happens as you read through this book. When you make a decision, you say, "We *will* do it."

What kinds of decisions and commitments are needed? First, decide *when* you will work together on the next chapter. Are you going to continue right now or come back to the book tomorrow? Two weeks from now is too far away! Decide now when you will continue by completing the next exercise.

Exercise: Making the Commitment

Write this sentence in your individual notebooks. Fill in the day, time and place as you write it:

"I agree to meet on _____ (day) at _____ (time) at _____ (place) for *one hour*."

Write this day, time and place in your personal appointment calendar as well so you remember to keep your commitment.

Two

Whose Fault Is It?

The couples you read about in chapter 1 clearly show that the conflict that money can cause in a relationship can result in tension, estrangement and hopelessness. To deal with these powerful emotions, most couples communicate in one of four ways. Most couples don't realize they are *choosing* a way of communicating, but they are—just like you and your partner. You respond to each other in the only way you think you can when you feel stress and anxiety.

Choice #1: "Let's Keep on Fighting"

If you and your partner have chosen this form of communicating about money, you continue to argue about how much to spend—whether on a haircut or a vacation, on a new suit or a new car, on a new house or the cost of lunch at work. You just keep fighting and arguing.

And, you continue to fight and argue over whose fault it is. Who is to blame for spending too much money? Which of you doesn't earn enough money?

In making this choice, couples must hope that their relationship can handle the tension, estrangement and hopelessness. Couples that communicate about money in this way sound like this:

- "How could you be so stupid!"
- "You have no discipline."
- "If you were smarter, you could earn more money."
- "If you really loved me, you would find a way to earn more money."
- "You just keep writing checks until you run out."
- "You just keep spending until our credit cards are at their limits."
- "What's the matter with you?"
- "It's all your fault."

Remember Julie and David, the first couple you read about in chapter 1? This couple communicates in this way when they have money disagreements.

When a couple consistently uses choice #1, they eventually get scared by what all the fighting is doing to their relationship. It's too dangerous to their relationship to keep fighting, and they decide that this choice no longer works for them.

Choice #2: "We're Tired of All the Fussing and Feuding"

If you have chosen this form of communicating about money, all the fighting and name-calling during money disagreements scares you. In fact, you're so scared that you or your partner has decided to take charge of the money. The partner not in charge has simply quit. So one of you makes all the money decisions while the other acquiesces. To stop the fighting, the acquiescing partner goes along with the money decisions even if he or she doesn't really agree.

The acquiescing member of the couple sounds like this:

- "You earn the money, so you make the decisions."
- "I don't know how to do this, so why don't you do it."
- "Just do what you want."
- "My opinion doesn't matter anyway, so you decide."
- "Money is ruining our life. I don't want to talk about it anymore."
- "Just tell me how much I can spend."
- "I'll just be quiet while you vent."
- "I'll make it; you spend it."

The take-charge, decision-making member of the couple sounds like this:

- "You're no good with numbers, so I'll make the money decisions around here."
- "It's my role in this family to make the decisions about money."

- "You won't do it anyway, so I might as well take over."
- "Because I said so. . . ."
- "I'm tired of all the arguing, so I'll decide from now on."
- "You're not disciplined enough, so I'll take over."
- "I'm the one who pays the bills, so I'll tell you what we can afford."
- "I'm the one who makes the most money, so I'll decide."

Neil and Anne communicate in this way when they have a conflict about money. Anne told Neil, "You figure it out."

Kate and Larry also fit into this model.

Couples that respond to conflict with this second choice of communicating eventually find that this choice doesn't work either. Sometimes one partner gets tired of acquiescing and pretending not to have any opinions about money decisions. Or, sometimes the acquiescing partner starts getting concerned about the money decisions made and is tired of being ignored or told what to do all the time.

In Maria and Jack's relationship, Maria got tired of anxiety-driven panic attacks. She became concerned about some of the money decisions Jack was making and began questioning him. Jack's response to this questioning was to tell Maria it was not her business. He told her to be quiet and let him make the decisions.

This choice of communicating also doesn't work because sometimes the partner making the decisions gets tired of the responsibility. Remember Will? At the age of forty-four he is feeling exhausted, discouraged and old. He's tired of carrying the financial responsibilities for the family. Moreover, his decisions are not working for them as a couple. College is looming. Job layoffs are possible. This choice of communicating is no longer working for Will and Diane.

When these first two choices of communicating are no longer workable, many couples make a third choice.

Choice #3: "The Sound of Silence"

As a way to avoid tension and misunderstanding, these couples decide to simply ignore the money part of their lives. Many times, this decision is by unspoken agreement. Couples believe that somehow, as long as the bills get paid and the kids are clothed, they can avoid talking about money. Since the couple isn't talking, individually they must hope that nothing really bad happens in their money life. One partner may notice that some of the bills are paid late or that they just aren't saving any money, but they still continue to hope nothing bad will happen. Even though they are going deeper into debt each month, they hope that somehow their money life will be all right. These couples simply accept these financial consequences in order to live without conflict.

Of course, silence doesn't work for long. Remember Denise and Ted? They tried silence as a way to protect their relationship. They were so angry and were being so mean to each other, they simply decided not to talk about money. They knew the arguing would eventually lead to divorce. But remember, silence didn't work for this couple. Financial decisions weren't being made. If Denise and Ted had not made an appointment, they would have eventually gone back to arguing and blaming. Nothing would have changed between them as a couple or in their money life.

When none of these three choices seem to work in a couple's

money life, some couples believe they have just one other alternative.

Choice #4: "Let's Just End This"

Naturally, couples get tired of fussing and feuding. They are exhausted by the tension, estrangement and hopelessness and also scared by these feelings. They're not able to get past the blaming. Their money life is not working. They know that:

- fighting about money doesn't work;
- one person taking charge doesn't work;
- not communicating about money doesn't work.

For these couples, the negative financial consequences continue to get worse. Debt increases, bills are paid late, savings are not building, and on top of all this, they don't like each other any more because of the fighting. Emotional and physical intimacy disappear.

A couple in this situation gives up and says, "That's enough. We quit. Let's end this relationship." This is what Shelly and Rob did. They couldn't find a workable way to communicate about money decisions, so they divorced. Shelly said it best when describing her feelings: "As hard as the divorce has been . . . I feel saner and safer than I ever felt married to Rob."

When all else fails, when couples just cannot live with the tension, estrangement and hopelessness, they make this fourth choice.

In my experience, most couples use a combination of the first three choices. You probably do, too. But all couples have a *primary* choice. This is their first response when they feel stress and anxiety about money. After couples have responded from their first choice, they usually move on to their second choice and then their third choice. Then when they get anxious about the effects of these changes in communication styles on their partnership, they move back to their first choice of communicating. And they start all over again. . . .

Your Turn

Review the four choices couples make when communicating about money and answer the questions that follow.

Choice #1: "Let's keep on fighting"

Choice #2: "We're tired of all the fussing and feuding"

Choice #3: "The sound of silence"

Choice #4: "Let's just end this"

- What is your *first* choice of a method of communicating about money as a couple? Which choice do you make when you start to feel stress and anxiety as you try to communicate?

- What kinds of statements do you each use when communicating with your partner?

- What is your *second* choice of a method of communicating? What do you each say to each other when you are responding from this second choice?

- What is your *third* choice of communicating? What do you say to each other when you are responding from this third choice?

- Have you ever thought about ending your relationship (choice #4) as a way to stop the stress? Have you and your partner ever talked about this? If so, what was happening at the time? What stopped you from starting divorce proceedings?

Well, I for one am glad you didn't go ahead with a divorce. I *know* you and your partner can communicate effectively about money, if you both are willing. I know this because as a couple, you have a fifth choice of communication.

Choice #5: Learning a New Way

Think back for a moment. Do you remember when you were first in love? Do you remember how careful you both were with each other? You really thought that you could work through any problem simply because you loved each other. Remember? Even problems involving money seemed solvable, and you believed that any disagreements could be worked out together, as a couple.

But as the months and years pass, the possibility of working out money disagreements can seem more and more naive and simplistic.

"You got that right, Ruth," Neil responds. Remember Neil? He earns a large income, and his wife, Anne, wants to save more money in case a catastrophe happens.

"Sure, we're going to work together," Neil says sarcastically, "just like we always have—by fighting every time I spend money or by me doing what Anne says or her doing what I say. We'll work together, all right."

Choice #5 means: *We have decided to learn a new way of working together in our money life.*

No one is saying this is easy. Whether your money disagreements are large or small, it is difficult to try again and learn a new way of working together. Whether your money disagreements are part of your daily life or happen only occasionally, this is a hard choice. But isn't all the fighting and fussing and feuding hard, too? Waiting for the next explosion with your partner is hard. Angry silence is hard. And hopelessness and frustration are hard, too.

So, "learning a new way" will be difficult. But isn't the difficulty worth it if there is a possibility that things could really change? Think about it. Your money life could really work! The information and ideas in this book have helped thousands of couples, many with a money life quite similar to yours. If it worked for them it can work for you, if you're just willing to use the information and the ideas.

Your Turn

- Think about how hard fighting about money has really been. Remember how angry, hurt, hopeless and discouraged you have felt. Have you wanted to run away from it all?

- Think about how hard fighting about money has been on your partner. Remember the hurt, the tears and the silence. Remember the mean things you said. Remember the name-calling.

- If you have children, think about how hard all this fussing and feuding has been on them. Remember the sadness you have seen in their eyes when there was silence between you and your partner. Remember the fear in their eyes when the two of you fought.

It's been hard, hasn't it? So, both of you already know you can do something that's hard. You've been doing it for months and maybe even years, just like Kim and Denny:

"Oh, we can do hard," Kim's voice is sad. "Denny and I really have been doing hard for years with all this fighting and anger and hopelessness. Not knowing if we're even going to stay married—that's hard."

"That's not even the *really* hard part," says Denny. "The children. You had to mention the children." Tears fill his eyes. "They're six and eight years old, Ruth. They're just little. I remember one night when I was hollering at Kim, and my eight-year-old ran into the room crying. He pulled on my arm and shouted, 'Stop it! Stop saying bad things to Mommy. Stop it!' I just pushed him away. I left the house and didn't come back until I knew everyone would be asleep."

Kim is crying as Denny talks.

"If we can't do this for ourselves," says Denny, "we need to at least do it for the kids. I'm ready, Ruth. I'm ready to figure out another way to talk about money. How about you, Kim?"

"It can't be any harder than what we've already done," Kim answers. "Sure, let's do it. Wouldn't it be great if we really could? You know, Ruth, I kind of like this guy sitting here and we have two great kids. It's just this money part that's so hard."

Your Turn

- What are you thinking right now? Maybe you're thinking that Kim and Denny are right—that maybe, just maybe, the two of you, like them, could learn a new way to work with money as a couple. What do you think?

To make your money life work as a couple, you must learn a new way to work with money. If you decide you want to learn a new way to work with your money as a couple, you must make sure you understand what you are agreeing to: If you are choosing to find a new way to work with your money as a couple, you are deciding to change.

The important word here is *deciding*. Without a clear decision, you won't be able to keep working with your partner when it feels really hard. Without a clear decision, you will go back to the responses that have not worked for you in the past.

You haven't made a decision if you just say, "Well, we sure hope this works." Or, "We can try it, I suppose, and see what happens." These statements do not reflect a clear decision to change.

A decision is a *commitment to action*. A decision is a *commitment to change*. You keep your commitment even when life gets hard. You keep your commitment even when you're tired, discouraged, resentful, hurt, disappointed or angry. If you have chosen to find a new way to work with your money as a couple, you have *decided to change*. You aren't just hoping or wishing you will change. *You have decided to change the way you work with your money as a couple.*

> **A decision is a *commitment to action*. A decision is a *commitment to change*.**

Exercise: Making a Commitment to Action

In your individual notebooks, write "Chapter 2" at the top of the page. Then write the following:

"I have decided to learn a new way of working with money in my relationship with _____ (your partner's name). I will keep my commitment even when the new way seems difficult. I will show my commitment to this change by continuing to work through this book with _____ (your partner's name)."

Put your signature under that statement and date it. This statement is a contract—a contract is a decision and it is binding. This contract is first with yourself and then with your partner. It represents your decision to change.

Now, each of you, read your decision to change out loud to your partner.

Changing Without Blaming

Congratulations! You have made a decision to change.

But wait. We need to add two additional words for this choice to be really effective: *Without blame*, we have decided to learn a new way of working together in our money life.

These two little words are essential to make this choice work. *Without blame* means that neither one of you is more at fault than the other in your money life. *Without blame* means that you share responsibility equally for whatever your present money situation is.

Remember David and Julie, from the beginning of chapter 1? David explodes in response to this information:

"Won't work," he argues. "I'm telling you, Ruth, that is the most ridiculously inaccurate, unrealistic, untrue statement I have heard in a long time.

"Do you really think I am going to accept the responsibility for Julie almost driving us into bankruptcy?" he asks. "It's not my fault. Julie does all the spending. All I do is earn as much money as I possibly can to try to keep us out of bankruptcy court. Give me a break! I won't agree to this because it's not my fault."

"Here we go again." Julie is angry now. "Same old song, over and over. It's not poor David's fault. It's all Julie's fault because the children need clothes and because David needs clothes. I get blamed because I'm the one who buys things for this family! It seems to me, David, that you are pretty happy with your life and your food and your newspapers and your suits and your vacations. No complaints there, right?"

Julie continues, this time her voice sounding tired, "Come on, David. You can't enjoy all the things we do and then blame me when we need to use the Visa card or when the mortgage is paid late. That's not fair."

Remember that choice #5 says you have decided to learn a *new way* of working together in your money life. Can you see from the exchange between Julie and David that it's nearly impossible to learn a new way unless you give up blaming each other?

Without blame means that you both understand that you cannot change the past, but you can decide you want a future together. *Without blame* means that this new way of working with your money is based on mutual respect. You each must accept that whatever your money problems are right now, whatever mistakes you both have made and whatever mean things you have each said, you share *equal* responsibility.

Without blame means that you both understand that you cannot change the past, but you can decide you want a future together.

Equal responsibility does *not* mean you have played identical roles spending and earning money. And equal responsibility does *not* mean you have made the same mistakes. Of course not.

Equal responsibility *does* mean that whatever the dynamics between you and your partner, you both share the responsibility for those dynamics. Maybe you express hurtful anger, like David and Julie. Or maybe you distance yourself from each other and feel hopeless, like Ted and Denise. Or, like Jack and Maria, maybe you feel panic and resentment about money.

Equal responsibility *does* mean that whatever the dynamics between you and your partner, you both share the responsibility for those dynamics.

The words *without blame* acknowledge that you share equally the responsibility for your money life, knowing that you have played different roles in how you got where you are today.

Without blame also means that you share equally the responsibility for the specifics of your money life right now:

- You're equally responsible if bills are being paid late.

- You're equally responsible if as a couple you do not earn enough money to pay all the bills.

- You're equally responsible for not having enough savings.

- You're equally responsible if your credit cards carry high balances.

- You're equally responsible if you have overdrawn your checking account.

- You're equally responsible if your retirement account is not adequately funded.

Again, equal responsibility for these financial areas of your life does *not* mean you have played identical roles or made the same mistakes. You have each played different roles in creating the money situation you are in. Your different roles have contributed to your money situation, and you share equal responsibility for that situation.

If I could, I'd create a stamp that says "50 percent" and stamp each of your foreheads. Then, as you go about your money lives—earning, spending and saving—you would be reminded as you look at each other that you each carry "50 percent" responsibility—that is, *equal responsibility*. When you're fighting about money, you would see "50 percent" stamped on your partner's forehead and remember that she carries a full 50 percent of the responsibility for this fight—no more and no less. When you look in the checkbook and see there is not enough money to pay the mortgage, you would look up at your partner and see "50 percent" stamped on his forehead and remember that he carries equal responsibility for your predicament—no more and no less.

Let's check in with David and Julie about this:

"So you're saying that David and I are both responsible for us not having enough money and for the debt?" asks Julie. "You're saying that it's not just my fault but he's at fault, too—just as much as me. Is that right?"

The answer, of course, is yes. Both partners in every couple are responsible—*equally*—for their money situation. Equal responsibility means that you both:

- share responsibility for not being able to communicate;
- share responsibility for blaming;
- share responsibility for the silence;
- share responsibility for not being able to make decisions together that make your money life more positive and workable.

You have each played different roles in creating an unworkable money life, and both of you are equally responsible for the financial results and for how it has affected your relationship.

"So," David interrupts, "Julie can't blame me for not making enough money, and I can't blame her for the Visa bill. Is that right?"

Again, the answer is yes. Blame is not the issue. We are forming a new model for your money life that is not based on blame. This new model is based on shared responsibility for the present money situation and shared responsibility for creating change for the future.

> **This new model is based on shared responsibility for the present money situation and shared responsibility for creating change for the future.**

It's interesting to watch a couple interact once they are willing to stop blaming each other. Each partner starts to feel regret about blaming the other for so long. Once they stop pointing fingers, both share regrets about how stuck they have been. Couples begin to understand how paralyzing that blaming has been in their money life.

David and Julie are beginning to see how this new model is based on shared responsibility for their present money situation and shared responsibility for creating change for their future:

"You're right, Ruth," says Julie. "No matter what happens, we begin by blaming each other, 'You should've done this!' or 'Why didn't you do that?' The blaming stops us from doing anything about the problem. We both just get mad."

David joins the conversation. "We always get stuck in the blaming. I think that's why, year after year, we never get ahead. I blamed Julie for the Visa bill four years ago and she blamed me for not earning enough money. Four years from now, if we don't change, I'll still be hollering about her driving us into bankruptcy and she'll holler at me that I should earn more. I get it!"

David is on a roll now. "If we stop blaming and say that we both have screwed up, or at least admit we have allowed ourselves to stay so stuck, then we both agree that we are equally responsible for being stuck. I can accept that. I will accept that I am 50 percent responsible for that Visa bill, if for no other reason than I've been stuck blaming Julie and we've never been able to figure out how we can get the darn thing under control. I get it! I accept my 50 percent responsibility."

"I can't believe what you just said," Julie says. "You just said you weren't going to blame me for the Visa charges any more. You just said you wanted to figure out a way for us to get it under control. You used the word 'we.' I can't believe it! Yes, Ruth, I agree to my 50 percent responsibility. I know that I can't blame David for not making enough money. I know we have to find a way to get a handle on our spending. I agree."

Look at what just happened here with David and Julie. With their commitment to find a new way of working with money—without blame—they each took a step closer to the other. Now, and only now, are they able to move forward and create a future together.

Your Turn

- Are you willing, like Julie and David, to learn new, more workable ways to talk about and work with your money?

- Are you willing to accept a full 50 percent of the responsibility for all that was said when you communicated about money?

- Are you willing to accept 50 percent responsibility for all that was done with the money?

Accepting 50 percent of the responsibility means that you accept that you have each played an equally important role in creating your present money situation. It means you want to stop where you are right now and start over—with new information, new ideas, new skills and a new way to talk about and work with your money.

If the old way had worked, you wouldn't be reading this book right now. You and your partner may disagree about *why* your money life isn't working. You may disagree about *what* is really wrong—whether too much spending or too little income. And, up to now, you may have disagreed about who is at *fault* for the problems in your money life.

Your money life is *not* about fault. Your money life is *not* about blame. It is about what *is*—and it's about what you want your lives to *be*.

> **Your money life is *not* about blame. It is about what *is*—and it's about what you want your lives to *be*.**

Remember, you have already made a decision to change. Now it's time to make another decision. It's time to decide that your new money life will be based on shared responsibility—starting now.

Exercise: Accepting Responsibility

Open your individual notebooks and write the following statement:

"I have decided to accept my 50 percent responsibility for how we talk about money and how we spend, save and earn money. Although we play different roles in our money life—spending, saving and earning—I am 50 percent responsible for our present money life."

Like last time, sign and date the statement. Once again, your signature and date symbolize that this is a commitment—a contract—and you intend to keep it.

You have made three important, life-changing commitments since you started this chapter:

1. You have decided to learn a new way of working together in your money life.

2. You have decided to learn a new way to talk about and work with your money. And, you decided to work through this book together as a way to keep that commitment.

3. You decided to remove the blame from your relationship by equally sharing with your partner the responsibility for your money life.

Congratulations! These are life-changing commitments. However, you need to make one more commitment before you stop for the day.

When will you meet to continue your work in this book? My recommendation is that you continue with chapter 3 right now. The chapter is about understanding how you got where you are today, and it will not take you very long to work through.

If you decide to continue right now, move on.

If you decide to wait a few days before continuing, complete the next exercise.

Exercise: Making the Commitment

Write this sentence in your notebook:

"I agree to meet on _____ (day)
at _____ (time) at _____ (place)."

Again, be sure to write this scheduled time together in your own personal calendar or appointment book. Be sure to make your other plans around this appointment with your partner.

Three

Let's Begin at the Beginning

Congratulations! You have kept your agreement to continue working together through this book. Part of learning to work with money differently is learning to trust each other to keep commitments—all commitments. Later in this book, we'll work more on building this trust between the two of you.

In chapter 2, you made this commitment to each other:

Without blame, we have decided to learn a new way of working together in our money life.

Learning a *new* way of working together means finding a way that is different from your old way. If you are like any of the couples you have read about in this book, the *old* way begins with a discussion—sometimes heated—about your personal money behaviors. You might begin with a "laundry list" of what each of you has done, or not done, with your money. According to the *old* way of working together, discussions probably centered on how much money you spent and what you spent it on. Or the money talk centered on how much money you were saving or earning.

As you begin a new way of working together in your money life, you won't start with a discussion of your money *behaviors*—your spending, saving and earning. If you start with a discussion of these money behaviors, you, like the couples described so far, will most likely start fussing and feuding all over again.

Remember, if you are reading this book, it means that somehow your money life together is not working as well as you would like. If you start a discussion by talking about the same money behaviors, nothing will change. You will simply see that once again you have not found a way to change your own or your partner's money behaviors.

Here's how David and Julie are stuck in a discussion about money behaviors:

"I know a solution—I've *always* known a solution to the money problems, Ruth," says David. "Just fix *her*. I mean, make Julie stop spending."

"Make *me* stop spending!" Julie interrupts. "Our money problems aren't my fault. If you'd just earn more money. . . ."

Do you see what I mean? David and Julie are back to where they were when we first met them in chapter 1. Nothing changes in their money life because they start at the same place in their money discussions. He says, "Stop spending." She says, "Earn more money." That's where they get stuck—time after time, year after year.

Nothing may be changing in your money life, either, because you start with the same familiar money problems. You and your partner have the same discussion—over and over again.

Your Turn

• When you and your partner talk about money, where does the conversation always seem to get stuck?

• At that stuck place, what do you say to your partner? What do you remember your partner saying to you?

• Tell each other, right now, how you each answered those questions. Do you two agree on the place that you get stuck?

• If you don't seem to agree, try again.

Getting Unstuck

Most couples truly know where they get stuck in a discussion about money. However, it can be difficult to identify that stuck place, because it's hard to admit you're in the same place, having the same conversation. We want to believe that a "heated" discussion is simply in response to something wrong our partner did. It's very discouraging to admit we are truly stuck—and have been for a long time.

Jack and Maria from chapter 1 are also stuck:

"Every time we talk about money," Jack explains, "we always end up with me saying, 'You're not supporting my business,' and Maria saying, 'We're going to lose our house.'"

Jack chuckles as he continues, "I always thought that Maria was stuck. She just couldn't get off the house thing and her fear. But since we both end up at the same place saying the same things, I guess I'll have to admit you're right. We both get stuck, and it gets so darn discouraging! We've got to find another way to talk about this. This is just nuts!"

Like Jack and Maria, you need to learn a new way to talk about money *so you don't get stuck*. You need to start talking about money from a totally different perspective—from a new place.

Instead of starting a conversation about money at the money behavior level, start at the *source* of the behavior itself. To do this, you need to understand both yourself and your partner in a new way.

First, you need to understand why *you*, individually, act the way you do with your money. As you can see, David is feeling some resistance about this:

"Oh, come on, Ruth," says David. "Julie simply needs to control her spending. If I really told the truth, I'd tell you that she needs to learn basic math so she can keep track of the money better in the checkbook."

"Don't start, David," Julie interjects.

This time *I* interrupt before they get any further into their own stuck place.

I suggested to them, and I suggest to you, that before we continue you may want to remind yourselves what you know for sure about each other. Say, out loud, to your partner:

"I know we are both intelligent, capable and competent people. We are both trying as best we know how to conduct our money life in a responsible manner."

Did you *both* repeat this statement? This is no time for reticence! You want to change your money life, right? You feel stuck, right? Then read the statement to each other, with special emphasis on the words *intelligent*, *capable* and *competent*.

That statement, by the way, is absolutely true. The reason you get stuck is not about intelligence, capability or competence—even though you may try to blame your money problems on your partner's lack of these three attributes. Lack of intelligence, capability or competence—in either one of you—is *not* the reason you make the money decisions you do and then argue about them later.

Earlier we talked about *money behaviors*. Money behaviors are the decisions you make about your money—your earning decisions, your spending decisions and your saving and investing decisions. The decisions you make in these three areas are controlled by your attitudes about money. I call these attitudes about money your *money beliefs*.

Identifying Your Money Beliefs

Learning a new way of working together with your money involves identifying your own money beliefs. These attitudes about money—the ways in which you think about money—are controlling your money behaviors.

> **These attitudes about money—the ways in which you think about money—are controlling your money behaviors.**

Another way to understand this concept is to think of your money beliefs as the manager of your money behavior. If you want to change your money behavior, you must change the way you manage your money. And to change the way you manage your money, you must identify and understand what money beliefs are in charge of your money behavior.

What are beliefs? Beliefs are an internalized emotional response to an experience. They are a feeling response to something that happened to you. You can probably guess how Jack would respond to the fact that we're talking about feelings—not just spending and saving, but feelings:

"You've lost me, Ruth," Jack says. "I get it that we don't want to be stuck—going round and round. But I really don't get this talk about beliefs and emotions. What we really need is a way to talk about money and debt and my business."

> **Beliefs are an internalized emotional response to an experience.**

I tell Jack I understand. Maybe, like you, he still wants to fix their money problems by starting at the same place—talking about the behaviors. But starting at this same place offers no hope of resolution for Jack and Maria, or for the two of you.

I ask Jack to trust me. The way he and Maria are conducting their money life is not working. We're talking about learning a new way to work with money. This new way really does work for couples. I know this, and thousands of couples I have worked with know this. Couples just as stuck as Jack and Maria, and just as stuck as you, have changed the way they work together with money.

Here's a simple analogy that will further clarify how this new method actually works: Let's say that one day you are out for a walk. About a block from your home, you hear a strange noise behind you. You turn around and see a dog running toward you, snarling and foaming at the mouth. In terror, you run to the nearest house and ring the doorbell, and your neighbor lets you in just as the dog reaches the door.

In the safety of your neighbor's house, and with your heart still racing, you ask your neighbor in a breathless voice, "Do you know what kind of a dog that was?"

Your neighbor answers, "That's a dalmatian."

Then you say, "Dalmatians are really scary, awful dogs."

You have just formed a belief about dalmatians. This belief is an emotional response to a real experience. And, this belief will absolutely, totally control your behavior around dalmatians.

Based on this new belief, what do you think you will *feel* the next time you see a dalmatian? Dislike? Fear, maybe. Possibly terror. You will have these feelings because you have a belief that says, "Dalmatians are really scary, awful dogs." This belief was formed by a feeling response to an emotional experience.

Based on this new belief, what do you think you will *do*—how will you behave—the next time you see a dalmatian? Most likely, you will try to avoid the dog. Actually, you will probably run away as fast as you can. You will probably move away if you see a dalmatian at a dog show or even if the dalmatian in your neighborhood is on a heavy-duty leash with a choke collar. Your emotional response—fear—and your physical behavior—running—will remain the same no matter where you see a dalmatian because of your belief that "Dalmatians are really scary, awful dogs." This new belief now controls your behavior.

Now, let's say that you and your partner are out for a walk one day and a dalmatian comes running toward you. You stop walking, grab your partner's arm and say, "We've got to get out of here. There's a really scary, awful dog coming toward us."

Unbeknownst to you, your partner's favorite pet as a child was a lovable and cute dalmatian. Your partner now looks at you and says, "What's the matter with you? Are you nuts? Dalmatians are the sweetest dogs on earth!"

And with that, your partner breaks away from you and walks toward the dalmatian to pet it. You, on the other hand, are still feeling fear, along with a little embarrassment. The embarrassed part of you wants to pet the dog, but the fearful part of you wants to run. Which part of you do you think will control what you do?

Your behavior will be controlled by the emotion you feel the strongest. Out of embarrassment, you may try to force yourself to move closer to your partner and the dalmatian, but because that initial fear response was so strong when you were chased by the dalmatian, your fear will most likely win—and you will run from the dog even if your partner looks at you with total bewilderment.

Now let's say that one day you decide you need to change how you act when you see a dalmatian. You decide this is important because, out of fear, you have not been walking as much as you used to and you miss the exercise. Knowing *why* you are afraid of dalmatians will make changing your behavior much easier. And if you understand that your fear came from a *real* and probably isolated experience, changing your behavior will be easier. You will be able to keep your focus on *changing* your fear rather than focusing on the results of that fear—your behavior itself.

If you don't understand why you are afraid, you will naturally feel embarrassed when your partner says, "What's the matter with you?" Out of embarrassment, you may respond to your partner with defensive anger, "There's nothing the matter with me. You're the one who petted a strange dog." Out of embarrassment, you may also respond with shameful silence as you ask yourself, "What *is* the matter with me?" Neither of these responses, of course, offers a solution to the problem.

David and Julie are beginning to see how this analogy applies to them:

"I get it!" David exclaims. "I really get it! Julie and I go around and around blaming each other as we criticize each other's behavior with money."

"Julie doesn't think I earn enough," he continues, "and I think she wastes the money I earn. So, what you're saying, Ruth, is that we are focusing on the wrong part of the problem if we really want to not fight so much. You're saying with this Dalmatian story that I need to understand why I blame so much—maybe why her spending scares me so much. . . ."

"And why I feel so judged and verbally abused by him," Julie interrupts. "Rather than hollering back at David, I need to understand why I get as defensive as I do and maybe even why I spend the money I do. Right, Ruth?"

Right.

Like Julie and David, you must learn that to change the way you work with money, you cannot start with the behaviors themselves—your actions with your money. Instead, you need to clearly identify what is controlling—what is managing—your actions with money.

Again, what is managing your behaviors with money are the beliefs that you hold about money. These beliefs absolutely control your money life—the way you spend, what you earn and what you save. Remember the dalmatian: The belief that "Dalmatians are really scary, awful dogs" absolutely controls your actions around dalmatians. If you want to change your money life, you must clearly identify what is managing your actions with money.

To start this process, you must clearly identify your own individual money beliefs. Remember that beliefs are an internalized emotional response to something that happened to you. Your money beliefs are an internalized emotional response to a money experience. I call these money experiences your money training.

> **Your money beliefs are an internalized emotional response to a money experience.**

So you will learn what your money beliefs are by recalling your experiences with money—your money training. As you allow yourself to remember your money training, you will be able to identify your emotional responses to that training. The stronger your emotional response when something happened to you, the stronger your beliefs are. These beliefs explain why you behave the way you do with your money.

Let's use the dalmatian analogy again. You may say to yourself, "Now I know why I get so scared every time I see a black-and-white spotted dog. I got scared—really scared—by a dalmatian that time on my walk. I really thought that dog was going to hurt me." This statement is your training. You may say, "I learned from that experience—that training—that dalmatians are really scary, awful dogs. There's nothing the matter with me," you may continue, "when I want to run away when I see a black-and-white spotted dog except that I have a good memory. I got scared and I remember that fear as a way to protect myself from getting hurt again."

Now, if you decide that you don't want to be scared any-more because you want the freedom to go for a walk, or if you decide you would like to share the enjoyment of dalmatians with your partner, or if you decide you are just sick and tired of this old belief—this fear—managing your life, then you are ready to change this old belief, and you can change your old behavior.

The commitment you made in chapter 2—to learn a new way of working together in your money life—involves chang-ing both your money beliefs and your money behavior as you learn how to be in partnership together. But first, so you really understand what controls your money behavior, you need to spend some time remembering your experiences with money—your money training—so you can identify your specific and individual responses to those experiences—your money beliefs.

"Oh, come on, Ruth!" Neil interjects. "Just tell us what to do to fix this mess we're in and let's skip all this feeling, emo-tional remembering stuff. I'm a busy man. Let's just get this money stuff fixed."

I ask Neil if he remembers what he told me at the begin-ning of their appointment. He told me about all the financial planning books he had read as he had tried to fix the money problems in his marriage.

As I remind Neil, Anne interrupts and says, "I didn't read any of those books. Neil just told me what I was supposed to do. I didn't do it. Those plans didn't work."

I continue by reminding Neil that I kept notes as he and Anne told me about some of the professional help they received over the past six years. According to my notes, they had worked with two accountants, four financial planners, one bank officer, one financial counselor in the employee assistance program through Neil's firm and two marriage counselors.

As I finish, both Neil and Anne are grinning. I suggest that maybe this time they will choose to start at the very beginning of the problem. Maybe this time, rather than starting with their behaviors, they will start with their own individual experiences and their own individual emotional responses to those experiences. Maybe this time, they will begin at the beginning so they can both individually and as a couple understand what beliefs they bring to their relationship. Then they can use this understanding to change their behaviors—and as a result change their money life.

"Well, none of the others really helped much, for very long," Neil acknowledges. "How about it, Anne? I'm ready if you are to figure this out."

Anne nods her head and says, "We're together on this one, Neil."

My hope is that you, too, will agree to begin at the beginning and take the time to individually explore the experiences and beliefs that you have brought to your relationship. If you do this, you will understand how you have created your present money situation. This is the goal of the next chapter, which you should each read on your own.

Exercise: Exploring Your Money Beliefs

On a new page in your individual notebooks, write "Chapter 3" and then the following statement:

"I am committed to take the time to begin at the beginning and explore my money training. I will begin this exploration in chapter 4."

You will explore your money beliefs individually, so before you go your separate ways and begin chapter 4, make an agreement with your partner about when you will meet again. You will need a few days or even a full week to explore your money beliefs individually. Complete the following exercise to decide when you will meet to share the results of this exploration.

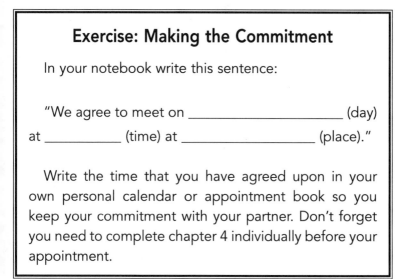

Exercise: Making the Commitment

In your notebook write this sentence:

"We agree to meet on _____ (day) at _____ (time) at _____ (place)."

Write the time that you have agreed upon in your own personal calendar or appointment book so you keep your commitment with your partner. Don't forget you need to complete chapter 4 individually before your appointment.

Four

First, I Need to Understand *Me*

To change your money life as a couple, you need to understand the attitudes—the money beliefs—each of you brings to your relationship. These money beliefs were formed by your personal experiences early in life. It's time now to explore these experiences so you can identify your own money beliefs. These experiences are your personal money history. They were your very first money training.

To explore your early money history, you'll need to mentally go back in time. Many of your most emotionally powerful experiences about money happened when you were quite young. They are powerful simply because money represents how we get what we want and need. When you were very young, you were dependent on someone else to get what you wanted and needed—whether food, clothes, love or security. From your emotional responses to this dependency, you formed strong beliefs about how to get what you wanted and needed in your life.

These beliefs that you formed so early in your life control your money behavior today. They control how you get what you want and need as an adult. They really do.

Remember what we learned in chapter 3 from the story of the Dalmatian: the more emotionally powerful the experience and the stronger the beliefs that come out of that experience, the more these beliefs control your behavior today. So, the more emotionally powerful the experiences you had as a child getting what you wanted and needed, and the stronger the beliefs you have about getting what you want and need today, the more these money beliefs control your money behavior. These behaviors can apply to how you earn money, how you spend money or how you save and invest money.

Exploring the Past

It's time to go back and explore these childhood experiences—those experiences that formed your adult money beliefs. These childhood experiences are your earliest money training.

The next exercise helps you identify specific, learned money beliefs that control and manage your present money life. This exercise calls for quiet contemplation—alone. When you meet with your partner again, you can decide what parts of your money history you want to share and what parts you want to keep confidential. Knowing that you have a choice about what you share will help you relax and remember the past as truthfully and clearly as you can.

As you answer the questions in the exercise, it is important that you remember your experiences from a child's perspective. Try to answer them by remembering what you felt as a young, dependent child. If you answer them from the perspective of an adult, you will learn more about the intellectual and rational part of you, which won't provide you with useful information. So remember, think and respond like a child.

Exercise: Exploring My Money History

On a new page in your notebook, write the words "Chapter 4, Exploring My Money History." Write your answers to the following questions on this page.

The first five questions in particular will help you to go back in time and remember what your life was really like as a child. Settle back and relax, and see what you can remember. Respond to the questions as the young child in you would respond.

1. How old are you? Pick an age when you were too young to earn money to buy things. Pick an age when you were totally dependent and yet old enough to remember.

2. What do you look like? Be specific so you get a clear picture of yourself at that time.

3. Where do you live? What town or city? What does your house or apartment look like?

4. What adults do you live with? Do you live with any other children? Who are they? How old are they?

5. What's the best part about living with these people in this home? Who is your favorite person

here? Why? Is there someone here you don't always like? Why? What's the hardest—or even scary—part about living with these people in this home? What do you wish you could change?

6. Do you ever make promises to yourself? Do you ever tell yourself what you would do, or not do, if you were an adult or the parent? (For example, do you ever say, "When I'm grown up, I'm going to . . ." or "When I'm big, I'm going to make sure I have . . ." or "If I were the parent, I would never . . ." or "If I were the parent, I would always. . . .") If you do make promises to yourself, what are the feelings you have inside as you make these promises? How strong are these feelings?

7. What happens in your family if you need something? Who do you tell if you need something like a costume for your first-grade play? What's the response? Let's say you are walking home from first grade and lose your shoe. How do you get another shoe? Whom do you ask? What's the response?

8. How do you get something you really want? Let's say your best friend just got a beautiful red bike, and you really want a bike just like it. Or maybe several of your friends are going to Cub Scout or Girl Scout camp. What do you do if you want to go too? If you ask someone if you can go, what's the response? If you don't ask, why not?

9. Do you have many friends? Name a couple of them. What do you like about each friend? What

do you dislike? Do your friends have about as much money as you do to spend? Do they have as many toys as you do? Do you feel like you fit in with your friends? If yes, what does it mean to fit in? If you don't feel like you fit in, are you okay with this or do you feel left out or bad about yourself? Do you wish you did fit in? Do you do anything to try to fit in?

10. Are you rich? How do you know? Are your friends or relatives or neighbors rich? How do you know? What are rich people like? Are they good or bad? Why? If you're not rich, do you want to be when you grow up? How much money do you think you need as a grownup to be rich?

11. Are you poor? How do you know? Are your friends or relatives or neighbors poor? How do you know? What are poor people like? Are they good or bad? Why? How do poor people become poor? What do they do? What don't they do?

12. What are your friends' parents like? Do they like you? How do they get along? Do they argue or fight? Is it different at your friends' homes than it is at your home? How? Which home makes you feel more comfortable? Why?

13. How much money does your family have? How do you know this? Who earns the money in your family? Does this person earn enough money for your family? What happens in your home to make you think this person does or doesn't earn enough money?

14. Who pays the bills in your family? How do you know this? Does this person do a good job? What happens in your home to let you know if this person is or isn't doing a good job paying the bills for the family?

15. Who spends most of the money in your family? Does this person do a good job making decisions for the family about how to spend money? For example, does this person make good decisions about how much to spend on groceries, when to buy new shoes or a new coat, how much to spend on birthdays or a vacation, or when to buy a new lamp? What do you hear and see that shows you what kind of job this person is doing?

16. Do you hear the adults in your family talk about money? If not, why do you think this is so? If yes, what do you hear? Remember specific conversations about money. How do you feel as you remember?

17. Do you think your parents like each other? How do you know?

18. As a child, what does the word *respect* mean? Do your parents respect you? Do they respect each other? Do other people seem to respect your parents? Do you respect your parents? Try to explain your answers to these questions.

19. Do any adults talk to you about money? If not, do the adults talk with any of the other children in the family? How do you know? If someone does talk to you, who is this person? What does this person

talk about with you? Why do you think this adult is talking about money with you? How does this make you feel?

20. Do you get an allowance? If so, how much? What are you expected to do with your allowance? Do your friends get an allowance? If you don't get an allowance, why do you think this is so? Do you have any money available to spend? Whether you get an allowance or have other money to spend, do you think you do a good job of spending it? How do adults respond to how you spend your money?

21. When do you get adult approval for who you are or what you do? When do adults tell you they are proud of you? How does it make you feel? When do you *wish* adults would notice you and what you do? When do you *wish* adults would tell you they are proud of you? Who, most of all, do you wish would show you that he or she is proud of you? Why?

22. Do you ever think or dream about being married someday—about being in a relationship with someone who loves you and whom you love? What do you think this relationship will be like? Don't be embarrassed. Tell the truth. Do you know anyone who has a relationship like the one you are thinking and dreaming about?

23. What does it mean to be safe? Be as specific as you can. What does it feel like? Do you feel safe? If yes, do you feel safe all the time? Where? (For

example, in your room or a tree house?) With a specific person? If not, why do you think you don't feel safe? Specifically, what needs to happen in your life for you to feel safe?

24. Who are five adults in your life right now, as a child? If you are a girl, name five women in your life. If you are a boy, name five men. Which of these adults seem to have a really good life—the kind of life you'd like to have when you're a grownup? Why do you think that person has a really good life? Which of these adults are married? Which of these married adults seem to have a really good relationship—one you'd like to have when you're a grownup? Why does their relationship seem so good to you?

25. Is there a question you think needs to be asked? If so, what is it? How do you answer this question?

You did it! You just completed your money history. You may not yet be sure what this history means to your present-day money life. We will work on what this history means in the next chapter. But before you move on to the next chapter, take a couple of minutes to look back at what you just wrote and then answer the following "Your Turn" questions.

Your Turn

• What question caused the strongest emotion as you answered it? What emotion did you feel? (For example, sad, mad, hurt, humor, joy, bittersweet.)

• Was there a second question that made you feel a lot of emotion as you answered it? What emotion did you feel?

• Which of your answers surprised you the most? You may have said to yourself, "I have never thought of that. . . ."

In chapter 5, you and your partner will exchange information about your money histories. Doing this will help you to understand each other. Before you move on, though, prepare yourself for your meeting with your partner by thinking about what you will say.

Write a summary of your money history—specifically focusing on the history that caused you the greatest emotional response or your most surprising memory. This summary does not analyze your history, rather it simply tells a story of your life. It is rather like a video camera playing back a recording of your life.

Make your summary fairly detailed and complete. It should take about ten minutes to read aloud.

When you have finished, continue on to chapter 5 at your next scheduled meeting together. Good work!

Five

Now, I Need
to Understand *You*

gain, I want to congratulate you for keeping your commitment to meet at the time you mutually agreed to meet. In chapter 7, you will learn how important this commitment really is. Trust, which is the cornerstone of any behavioral change in your money life, is earned when you do what you said you were going to do. For now, though, understand that each time you keep your commitment to meet, you are nurturing and building trust between you.

It's time now to read your summary of your money history to your partner. I'd like you to follow specific steps and time limits when sharing this information. Without time limits, one of you may feel discounted, or one of you may feel like you are listening to an endless story. These steps will help you both feel safe in sharing this information. By safe I mean you will both know the rules, and you won't feel judged or criticized or evaluated by your partner when sharing your information. You have probably each done plenty of that in the past. But remember, you have decided to communicate in a new way.

Exercise: Exchanging Money Histories

Decide which of you will read your summary first. Then, follow these steps:

1. The person reading has ten minutes, no more or no less. The easiest way to track this is to set a timer. If you finish reading before ten minutes are up, go back and give some examples from your childhood. When the timer sounds, you need to stop.

2. The person listening cannot interrupt the speaker. Absolutely. You cannot ask questions and you cannot groan. No rolling your eyes, yawning, reading the newspaper, answering the phone or talking with a child. Even if you believe you have heard all of this before, you have decided to respectfully listen to your partner. So actively listen—that means look like you're listening, and pay attention!

3. When the person reading is completely finished, the "listener" says, "Let me summarize what I just heard you tell me." The listener then summarizes his or her partner's childhood history, making sure to simply repeat what was heard. Don't analyze, and don't judge. This should be just like a video

---

playback. You have five minutes to repeat what you heard. You must talk for the full five minutes. Again, set a timer.

4. When the five minutes are up, ask the first speaker, "Did I miss anything?" The first person has three minutes to clarify what was missed. Set the timer for three minutes.

5. Now switch roles and start all over again.

Congratulations! You have just summarized the childhood experiences that make up your personal money training. And as you've already learned, this money training is the basis for your money behavior now, as an adult. It's this training that caused you to form your money beliefs, and it's these beliefs that govern your behavior today.

The money history is designed to help you understand what you learned as a child about getting what you want and need, about safety and security, and about belonging. This training formed your personal belief system—your money beliefs.

In chapter 6 you will explore how these money beliefs specifically affect your money behaviors. First, though, you both need to clearly identify your money beliefs.

Identifying Your Money Beliefs

At the end of the last chapter, you identified what question in the money history caused the strongest emotion as you answered it. For you to understand the importance of what you identified, remember that beliefs are an internalized emotional response to an experience. Just like feelings, beliefs can be irrational. And just like feelings, beliefs can be embarrassing. But feeling and beliefs are real and can control your behavior, including your behavior in your money life.

In the next exercise, you will review your strongest emotional response to the questions about your childhood experiences. These emotional responses will help you clearly understand the beliefs that govern your money behaviors.

Exercise: Identifying Your Strongest Emotional Responses

On a new page in your individual notebooks, write "Chapter 5" and then do the following:

1. Write down the three questions from the personal money history that created the strongest *emotional* response in you.

2. As you answered each of these questions, what were the emotions you felt?

3. You drew a conclusion from the emotion you felt—this is a learned belief. Still working individually in your notebook, put what you learned into words. What did you learn emotionally from each experience?

Remember Jack and Maria from chapter 1? Jack was starting a new business, which was causing Maria a lot of anxiety:

"Do you know what I learned, Ruth?" Maria says. "I learned that no matter how hard a woman scrimps and no matter how hard she works, she can still lose her home. My mother and father lost my grandparents' farm in foreclosure. My mother never recovered. I remember her crying all the time and telling my father it was his fault. We moved in with my father's parents. It was horrible for my brother and me."

Jack looks at his wife. "We're quite a pair, Maria. I remember my dad—even when I was a little kid—coming up with scheme after scheme to make money without having to get up and go and work at 5:30 every morning. He hated his job. When my brother Tim was born—he was number four—it seemed like my dad quit trying. I think he gave up because he knew with all the kids, he would have to keep working. My dad had a heart attack at work and died. He was forty-nine."

Jack continues, "I learned that if you want something, go get it. You could be dead tomorrow."

Like Jack, do you know what *your* beliefs are? Identifying them is an important step in the process of changing your money life. If you're still not sure what your beliefs are, let's try looking at them from a different direction. In the next exercise, we'll try identifying some of your beliefs and then connecting them *back* to your experiences. If you feel you already know what your money beliefs are, this exercise will confirm that you've identified them all clearly.

Remember, beliefs feel like the truth. If any of the beliefs listed in the next exercise sound true to you, then it's one of your personal money beliefs. Don't worry if the statement is politically correct. It won't be. Remember, beliefs are emotion-based, not intellectually based. If your belief feels embarrassing, it's because it is so different from how you want to see yourself or how others see you.

Before we move on to the exercise, let's check in with Larry and Kate from chapter 1. Larry is the financial planner who has had trouble planning his own retirement, and Kate is discouraged:

"Here I am," Kate says, "a strong, intelligent, upper-level manager at a well-known international company. I'm considered a role model for women coming into the company. And, as embarrassing as it is, I've identified my primary belief as 'Women will take care of the relationships, men will take care of the money.'"

"See, I told you it's embarrassing," she continues. "I just want Larry to handle the money decisions. Oh, I'll bring home my paycheck, but then I just want to be the 'little woman' and be taken care of. Talk about politically incorrect!"

Kate is beginning to understand the disparity between what she believes and what she thinks she *should* believe.

"The 'aha' for me," Kate continues, "is that's why I go silent when Larry starts venting. I figure if he can just get it out of his system, then we can go on with our lives—he takes care of the money and I take care of the home and family. But, until lately, I really haven't paid much attention to what he said. I've always thought that it really had nothing to do with me. It wasn't my responsibility. Interesting."

If you want to understand why you act the way you do with your money, or, as with Kate, how you act when money is discussed, you must identify what beliefs are controlling that behavior. Kate now understands why she stays so silent. Even though Kate manages a very large budget at work, at home she believes that managing the money is not her job.

Exercise: Identifying Money Beliefs

Read the following list of money beliefs. If any one seems ridiculous or puzzling to you, ignore it. It is not your belief. If any of the statements seem true and make sense, write them down in your notebook. Change any wording so the statement really fits you. Do this individually.

1. There's never enough money—ever.
2. I trust God to take care of me.
3. Money involves just one financial crisis after another.
4. No matter how much money I earn, someone always needs more.
5. There is no way to get ahead. It never works out.
6. I can't. . . .
7. If I want something, I deserve to get it.
8. I'm compulsive with money.
9. People around me are compulsive with money.
10. It'll work out. It always has and always will.
11. Why use your own money when you can use someone else's by borrowing?
12. Whoever earns the most money has the bigger say about how the money should be spent.
13. Money is the root of all evil.
14. Information about money is in the hands of only a few people—mostly the rich.
15. People around me are the problem.

16. I could be successful with money if I wasn't married.

17. I never get what I want. Others get what they want.

18. People take advantage of me.

19. I never have any real fun with money. Life is always hard.

20. I feel like I need to hide how much money I have and not be showy.

21. I'm scared to try to balance my checkbook.

22. I'm scared to pay bills—what if there's not enough—what if I need the money for something else that comes up?

23. No amount of money in the bank makes me feel safe.

24. No matter what we have and how much I earn, it could all go away tomorrow.

25. I'm not disciplined enough to be good with money.

26. Women are the emotional caretakers. Men are the wage earners.

27. I have never been good with numbers.

28. Money is power and power means abuse.

Make sure you don't limit yourself to this list. Do you have a belief statement that isn't on this list? If you do, write it down.

The statements in this exercise are *all* beliefs. Remember, beliefs feel like the truth. Your beliefs about how to get what you want and need are your money beliefs. Now, go back to your money history and the three most emotionally powerful childhood experiences you had. How were the belief statements that you just identified formed from those childhood experiences?

You are now being a detective about your life experiences and the resulting emotional responses to those experiences—your beliefs. How is your detecting going? Are you clear about what your three most powerful beliefs are? Have you written them down? Good for you.

If you are not quite sure about your beliefs, there's one more way to help you identify them. This time you will identify your beliefs simply from the *emotional response* you feel when you need to complete a money task or have a discussion about money.

Here are three emotions, along with a corresponding belief:

Emotion	Corresponding Belief
Resentment	I shouldn't have to do this. . . .
Defiance	But I don't want to. . . .
Fear	I can't. This is too hard. . . .

Do any of these three emotions feel familiar? If so, go back to your notebook and write down your personal belief that correlates with the emotion. Now, look again at your three most emotionally powerful childhood experiences. How were these emotions and the correlating beliefs formed from those experiences?

Continue to be a detective trying to uncover your money beliefs. Identifying these beliefs is critical. It's important that you understand how your actions are controlled by an emotion that is very real.

Your Turn

- Tell your partner your three learned money beliefs.

- Ask your partner to tell you his or her three learned money beliefs.

- Are you able to listen to each other without judgment?

- Are you able to understand your partner as well as you understand yourself?

- Do you have any questions of each other? Remember, your goal is to understand each other and not to judge.

Amazing! You two really *are* different, aren't you? Of course you already knew that. Your differences are probably what attracted you to each other initially. But now, your differences are probably what's been causing such frustration in your money life.

Our purpose in this chapter has been to clarify your individual beliefs and then to communicate them. As you communicated your beliefs, you have needed to remember that what is true for you is not necessarily true for your partner, and vice versa. You are both intelligent, capable and competent adults, and you will have different personal beliefs about money. You have been practicing a pure, simple and clear exchange of information, without judgment, criticism and blame.

You are another step closer to understanding your money life as a couple. In chapter 6, we'll explore the effects these money beliefs have had on your money life together. But before you go, make a commitment to meet again.

Exercise: Making the Commitment

In your notebook, write this sentence and fill in the blanks:

"I agree to meet on _____ (day) at _____ (time) at _____ (place)."

Once again, be sure to write the day and time in your personal appointment calendar.

Six

So, That's Why We Do That!

- Why do we spend more money than we have?
- Why don't I know the balance in my checkbook?
- Why do we put money into savings only to take it back out to pay bills?
- Why do we argue so much about money?
- Why can't we stay within our budget?
- Why can't we put more money away for retirement?
- Why do we keep charging things even when we say we won't?
- Why is it so hard to pay the bills on time?
- Why don't we ever get ahead in our checkbook?
- Why does money just seem so hard?

These are all questions about money behavior—what you do or don't do with your money, and what you say and don't say to your partner. They are questions about couple communication and couple action.

So far in this book, you have been working together to develop an understanding of *why* you do what you do with your money. You have been working to develop an understanding of *why* you talk—or don't talk—to each other the way you do about money.

You've begun to realize that your financial partnership is limited by your individual money beliefs you learned at an early age. With the best of intentions to create a financially healthy life, you create your present money life based on these beliefs—based on what you were taught as children. You repeat the same behaviors, just like the other couples profiled in this book, and, until now, you haven't been able to understand why.

Now you know why! You now know that your money behaviors are based on the money beliefs that you identified in chapter 5.

In this chapter, we want to explore the price you have paid in your money life. You will look at all the "why?" questions about your money behavior.

The Consequences of Your Money Beliefs

"Oh, come on, Ruth," says David, "we're getting just a bit too simplistic, aren't we? You're talking about the price Julie and I are paying in our financial life because of the way we were raised? I just don't see. . . ."

"I do!" Julie interrupts. "I really do! David, remember my number-one belief, 'There's never enough money, ever.' And there isn't. There never has been. My second belief is, 'If I want something, I deserve to get it!' And my third belief is, 'I've never been any good with numbers.' Don't you see, David? I'm really embarrassed to even admit this, but the way I handle money and all the fights I have with you are based on these three beliefs."

"But you always figure out a way for there to be enough money, Julie." David's voice is edged with sarcasm now. "By charging. You just keep charging and charging and charging."

I interrupt them at this point and ask David to be careful not to get sarcastic or critical.

You will want to be careful here, too. It's easy to be disrespectful during this part of the process. You may feel vulnerable because you're revealing the logical behavioral results in your money life that are based on the irrational, emotionally based beliefs you learned. Verbalizing this new self-understanding may feel quite embarrassing. So be careful with each other. This is a necessary step if you truly want to change your money life.

You may feel not only embarrassment but also anger as you listen to each other. Anger results when you allow yourself to remember all the painful money history you have shared. If you're not careful at this stage, you may show that anger to your partner as disrespect. Please stop yourself from doing this.

Anger results when you allow yourself to remember all the painful money history you have shared.

I tell David that the critical attitude he is expressing comes not just from disapproving of Julie's behavior but also from the beliefs he learned as a child from his father. David looks confused by this statement, so I ask him, "What are the three money beliefs you identified in the last chapter?"

"My three beliefs," David answers, "are first, 'No matter how much money I earn, someone always needs more. There's never enough money.' Second, 'My wife is the problem. I could be successful with money if I weren't married.' Bingo! Right, Ruth? And just for the final topping, my third belief is, 'My wife is compulsive with money.'"

I ask David what experiences from childhood formed those beliefs. He explains that his father was an angry, verbal man who had his own business. David was the oldest of six children. His mother was used to having nice things. Her relatives always talked about her "marrying down." The relatives also said his mother would drive them all into the poorhouse because of her spending. David's father eventually lost his business to bankruptcy and blamed his wife. His parents divorced after David left for college.

I look at David and say, "A lot of the emotions in that history—the beliefs in that history—seem very familiar with what you and Julie are experiencing in your present married life. Do you agree?"

"I think you're right," David agrees. "It's uncannily familiar. It's almost a little frightening how much my father and I are alike."

"It's not that you and your father are necessarily the same," I tell him. "I'm sure that if we wanted to, we could find more ways that you're different than you are similar to your father. And Julie may have some similarities to your mother. But she's more different than similar."

What's important here is to realize that David and Julie, like all other men and women, learned from their parental home an emotional way of responding to life. We've identified these patterns of response as money beliefs. These beliefs directly affect their perceptions of what happens in their lives.

When Julie spends more than David thinks she should, the fear-based belief he learned from his father says, "My wife is going to drive me to bankruptcy. My wife's spending is a threat to my well-being." Instead of having a rational, concrete and productive conversation about how they can both get what they want and need, David attacks Julie verbally—out of his fear—in an attempt to protect himself. He's afraid he will end up like his father, and he's trying to stop that from happening.

I ask David what he thinks about this.

"That does makes sense," David responds. He looks at Julie and says, "I didn't mean to, as Ruth called it, attack you. Sorry about the sarcasm."

Julie had been watching David very carefully during the conversation. Now she looks quite hesitant and unsure of herself. I ask her if she's willing to take a risk again and explain to David what she has learned about her money beliefs and how it has affected her behavior.

"Sure," Julie answers. "I do feel vulnerable when I talk with David about my spending. It doesn't take much for me to feel defensive and then begin verbally attacking him for not earning enough. My defensiveness doesn't change my money behavior, however."

"You know," she continues, "after listening to David's beliefs and my beliefs, I am absolutely astounded how they fit together. David said it was uncanny how his life now resembles his life as a child. I think it's uncanny how our beliefs seem to feed off each other. No wonder we've had such trouble with money."

Julie looks very thoughtful as she continues. "Let me try to explain. I believe there's never enough money. The way I try to make sure there is enough money is by charging. Charging creates more money, in a sense. Except the charge bills must be paid, which means we have even less money, so I charge even more to make there be enough money for today and. . . ." Julie pauses.

"David believes there is no way he can ever earn enough money for us," Julie continues. "So, he always feels behind, and we really *are* behind because of the charging. I get it! Because of our feelings—which you call our money beliefs—we behave in a way that makes our feelings true—which supports our money beliefs. It's a catch-22. My other belief is that if I feel like I deserve something, or that my children deserve something, I get it. I will not be deprived. And neither will my children."

Again Julie pauses. "But now I get it. I really do. I spend so I don't feel deprived, and there isn't enough money to take care of my deprivation, so I charge. And my third belief, which is that I'm no good with numbers, means, of course, I can't keep track of what I've charged, so the bills are always a surprise. David keeps earning money, but it's never enough to pay for everything."

David is obviously listening to Julie.

"It really is mind-boggling, Julie," David says. "I'm still a bit stunned that these simple beliefs—this stuff that we learned way back when we were kids—so completely control our lives. Part of me is really angry at the absurdity of it all. But I also feel sad at the blind, stupid waste of all these years."

Moving Beyond Regret

Anger and sadness are always part of new understanding. This is called the *regret stage*. The regret stage is a necessary part of every change. Couples in this stage of changing their money lives often say, "If only we had known . . . we could have done things differently."

> **The regret stage is a necessary part of every change.**

Regrets can be about the amount of pain and estrangement you have both felt. Regrets can be about the amount of time you have lost. They can be about the amount of money you have wasted. They can be about the hurt your children have felt. Regrets can be about anything.

The regret stage is healthy and necessary. It is a stage you need to go through if you are really going to change. In this stage, it's necessary to face the loss, feel the pain, accept the pain and allow yourself to move forward with hope for the future.

The truth is, until now, you didn't know *why* you were stuck, so you really couldn't have done anything differently. But now you've learned why you get so stuck in your money conversations and money behavior. Now you know, so it's time to do things differently. As soon as David and Julie can leave this regret stage behind, they will move into the new stage of change and hope.

"That's what I want," says David. "If it's this simple, then maybe we can really change how Julie and I work together with money. Oh, I get it that it will be hard, too. But, maybe, just maybe, Ruth, we can change."

I reassure Julie and David, just like I'd like to reassure the two of you, that yes, it really is this simple. Understanding *why* you do what you do with your money is really this simple. Individually and as a couple, you have been working on understanding why you do what you do in your money life. You've seen the understanding that David and Julie came to. Now, it's your turn.

Exercise: Understanding the Price You've Paid for Your Beliefs

At the top of the next clean sheet of paper in your notebooks, individually write "Chapter 6, The Price I've Paid for My Beliefs."

1. Copy the three beliefs about money you identified in the last chapter, leaving plenty of space between them for you to write.

2. Under each of your money beliefs, write: "My personal money behavior that has resulted from this belief."

3. Now, for each of your money beliefs, take the time to think about the specific relationship between your money belief and your money behavior. Write out your thoughts under each of your money beliefs.

4. When you have both finished, go ahead to the following exercise.

Exercise: Sharing What You've Learned

It's time to tell your partner what you've learned about the relationship between your money beliefs and your money behavior. As in chapter 5, we want to create safety from criticism, judgment, anger, rejection and sarcasm. To do this, follow these steps:

1. Decide who will go first.

2. If you are the person talking, you have ten minutes to explain what you have learned. As in the last chapter, set a timer.

3. The person listening cannot interrupt the speaker. Remember, listen actively—no yawning, no rolling your eyes, no answering the phone, no answering the door, no child care. Through body language, the listening partner shows interest and respect. Without interest and respect, this process won't work. Out of fear of a disrespectful response, the speaking partner will not be as honest.

4. When the time is up, the listening partner has five minutes to "play back" what he or she heard the speaker say. Again, set the timer.

5. The first speaker has three minutes to clarify, if needed.

6. Now switch roles and start all over again.

After you and your partner have each had a chance to explain what you've learned about the relationship between your money beliefs and your money behavior, take a moment to think about the information your partner just told you. Ask yourself, How do my money beliefs connect with my partner's money beliefs?

> **Ask yourself, How do my money beliefs connect with my partner's money beliefs?**

Remember Julie's comment earlier in this chapter: "I am absolutely astounded how they fit together. David said it was uncanny how his life now resembles his life as a child. I think it's uncanny how our beliefs seem to feed off each other. No wonder we've had such trouble with money."

Talk to your partner about how your money beliefs interconnect. Remember, do this without blame. In chapter 2 you agreed that whatever dynamics between you and your partner, you both share the responsibility for those dynamics. This means *no blame*. Based on your individual money beliefs, give each other your understanding of how the dynamic between the two of you actually works.

When Jack, who was getting his own business started, looked at his money training, he remembered his father trapped in a job and not being able to have his own business. Jack formed a belief that said, "I'm going to have my own company. I don't care what it takes. No one is going to stop me." And so he is.

When Maria, Jack's wife, looked at her money training, she recalled how her family lost their farm and had to move in with her grandparents. She formed a belief that said, "We could lose everything tomorrow because the husband doesn't know what to do. And no matter how hard I work, there's nothing I can do to stop it." Maria earns as much as she can, but it's not enough. So she lives with anxiety and panic attacks.

When Jack and Maria talked about how their money beliefs and behaviors interconnected, Jack began to see how Maria's beliefs created such fear in her.

"It's an epiphany, Ruth!" Jack exclaims. "Such a revelation! Nothing has really changed, but at least I understand why Maria gets so scared. And, I understand why I so bullheadedly just keep going forward, without listening to anyone."

"I understand," Jack continues as he watches Maria nodding her head. "I understand and I'm determined that we're going to change. Right, Maria? No one should feel as isolated as I do or as scared as you do. We will change!"

So spend a few minutes talking about how you see *your* individual beliefs interconnecting with your partner's. Continue to talk about the price you each have paid and the price your family has paid as a result of these beliefs and behaviors.

The rest of this book will help you, like Jack and Maria and like Julie and David, change the money beliefs and the money behaviors that have kept you both stuck. These changes are possible now because of the new understanding between you.

Exercise: Making the Commitment

Before you finish today, write this sentence in your individual notebooks and fill in the blanks:

"I agree to meet on _____ (day) at _____ (time) at _____ (place)."

Write the day and time in your personal calendar or appointment book.

Seven

We're on the
Same Side

In chapter 2, you and your partner made this commitment: "Without blame, we have decided to learn a new way of working together in our money life."

This commitment gives you the motivation you need to schedule times to meet with your partner and continue working through this book.

This commitment provides the willingness to explore your personal history and the money beliefs that result from that history. You now have the ability to come to a new understanding—first of yourself and then of your partner.

There are four cornerstones that anchor your new money structure. With this commitment, you have the first of the four cornerstones:

1. **Commitment**

2. **Trust**

3. **Respect**

4. **Compromise**

This new money structure will help you to create *new* behaviors with your money.

Commitment: The First Cornerstone

As you start building your new money structure, you need to renew your commitment to each other. You need to make sure this first cornerstone is in place, because change can be hard. Changing the way you communicate takes time. And changing your actions with your money can be quite difficult. We're talking about a simple, workable process of behavioral change, yet this process can be difficult.

Many adults believe that change is easy. Or, we believe that change just sort of happens—effortlessly. If you have identified a belief that says, "Somehow it will work out" or "I trust someone or something outside of myself," you may be one of these adults. I've told some couples that the work we do together is simply a "backup plan" to winning the lottery. After they chuckle, I tell them that, seriously, many, many women and men believe they really won't have to make difficult changes in their money lives. They believe that something will happen to make the process shorter and easier—something will fix their money lives.

Each of the couples profiled in this book, to one degree or another, hoped for this. But guess what? Each and every couple had to put the cornerstones of a new money structure in place. They had to develop new beliefs, new communication skills and new money skills. Just like you will.

It is true that change can be hard. Change takes effort. But deciding to put forth the effort to create change in your money life is the only way you can create real, lasting change. You can create lasting change if you are willing to make a commitment to this effort—even when it becomes hard.

> **Deciding to put forth the effort to create change in your money life is the only way you can create real, lasting change.**

Real-life changes usually bring hope, joy and new opportunities. But they can also be difficult. Parenting a child takes effort, and it can be hard at times. Starting a small business takes effort, and it can be frustrating. Moving into a new home in a new neighborhood can be a wonderful change, but it is also a difficult adjustment. Going back to school to get an advanced degree can be stimulating but also a struggle.

Getting married is usually a joyous occasion, but staying married can be a challenge. Marriage can be difficult even as it is wonderful—especially as a couple starts to work together on money. Real-life changes take commitment to make them work.

Are you both willing to recommit to creating real and lasting change in your money life as a couple? Are you willing to stay committed even if you feel frustrated? Will you stay committed even if it gets hard for you individually or as a couple? Even if your progress is not as fast as you had hoped?

Exercise: Recommitting to Creating Change

In your individual notebooks, write at the top of the next clean sheet of paper, "Chapter 7, My Recommitment to Creating Change." Then write the following statement and fill in the blanks:

"Without blame, I, _____, am committed to working with you, _____, to turn our money life around. I am committed to creating real change in our money life—both in how we communicate and in how we actually work with our money—even when it gets difficult."

Sign this commitment. Then, read the statement aloud to your partner, and have your partner do the same.

Remember, this commitment is a binding contract between you and your partner. This commitment, based on your new understanding of each other, will give you the ability and the motivation to create real change in your money life.

Now it's time to take action! You need to create a time and place to consistently work together on money. I want you to make a commitment to have a *weekly money meeting*. The commitment you have already made is necessary for you to take the risk of scheduling a set time and place to talk about money. Without that commitment, you probably won't show up for the meeting even if you schedule it.

Remember Denny from chapter 1? He and his wife, Kim, had come to see me on the advice of their marriage counselor:

"You got that right, Ruth!" says Denny. "Why would I show

up for a meeting when all I'll hear is how I'm spending money wrong? I'll just hear about how selfish I am and how I'm risking our financial security! Why would I do that? I'm not a glutton for punishment!"

Like Denny, you may have memories of painful discussions with your partner and would prefer to avoid a weekly money meeting. Of course! Intelligent men and women always look for ways to avoid pain. And you are an intelligent person. But you now know that avoidance doesn't solve anything— except temporarily. Avoidance can create greater pain in the long run. And besides, you have made a commitment to learn a new way to work with money. As part of that commitment you must agree to meet weekly.

Scheduling this weekly money meeting might be easier if you truly understand why it is so crucial to taking charge of your money as a couple. The weekly money meeting has two primary purposes.

First, all change starts with a symbol. The weekly money meeting is a symbol of your commitment to creating real change in your money life. The meeting is a specific action that shows you are both moving beyond words, beyond understanding and beyond your present money beliefs toward real change.

Just as the commitments to meet again that you made at the end of each chapter have made a difference in your understanding of each other, so making an *ongoing* commitment to meet will make a difference in your actual money life. Keeping this commitment, week after week, will anchor the second cornerstone of your new money life: Trust.

Trust: The Second Cornerstone

Trust doesn't come automatically with love, even though it would be much simpler if it did. Trust doesn't come automatically with the passage of time. In fact, for many couples, any trust they once felt erodes over time as they fuss and feud over money.

You know how trust works. You really do. Trust is formed over time—day after day, week after week—by consistently keeping your commitments to each other. Keeping this commitment to a weekly money meeting week after week—no matter what—builds trust.

> **Trust is formed over time—day after day, week after week—by consistently keeping your commitments to each other.**

Building trust also helps you to change some of your money beliefs. Look back at your three strongest money beliefs. Without even knowing you, I'm sure that your beliefs have something to do with trusting—trusting yourself and/or trusting your partner. Keeping your commitment to meet week after week will help you change your money beliefs that say, "I can't trust myself" or "I can't trust you."

You must keep your commitment even if the money meeting is hard to fit into your schedule. You must meet even if you are not feeling well, even if your child is ill, even if the two of you are fighting and even if your in-laws are visiting. This commitment says that you will make every effort to meet, and if you absolutely can't, you will reschedule the meeting within twenty-four hours—at the convenience of your partner. After all, this is a key meeting and you cannot just skip it.

Remember, all real change takes effort. All real change takes commitment. Sometimes it is hard. And, as a symbol of your commitment to change your money life, you have decided to have weekly money meetings.

The second main purpose of the weekly money meeting is that it provides a *place* for you to accomplish money change. This money change begins with learning how to communicate about money as a couple. The weekly meeting is the place where you'll learn how to communicate in a more workable and effective manner.

Couple communication takes a willingness and a desire to communicate. You have already showed this willingness by making commitments in earlier chapters. Couple communication also takes a set of skills that you do not now have. You don't have these skills either because no one ever taught them to you by their example or because you may not have had a strong desire to learn them in the past.

How do I know you don't have these couple communication skills even when I don't even know you? Simple. If you had workable and effective couple communication skills, you wouldn't be reading this book. You wouldn't be having problems in your money life together. This meeting time is a place to practice, week after week, these new communication skills.

The weekly money meeting is also the place to practice more effective ways to actually structure your money. It is a place where you both are mentally prepared to make money decisions. A "stressor" for many couples is being asked to remember financial information, such as what something cost or whether a specific bill was paid, when you are not prepared for the question.

This scenario is familiar to Diane and Will, who are the couple that seems so frustrated about not getting ahead:

"He always does that," says Diane. "We finally get the kids to bed and can relax and he says something like, 'What did that new bedspread cost?' Or 'How much will the next Visa bill be?'"

"Well, you do it, too," interrupts Will. "I just get home from work and you say, 'We got an overdraft notice, what should I do?' Or, I'm leaving for work and you say, 'Did you pay the car insurance?'"

All couples do this. All couples ask for financial information when the other person is not prepared. At the weekly money meeting, you will both be mentally prepared to exchange financial information. If the information is not readily available, you can bring it to the next meeting—just one short week away.

In your weekly money meeting you will learn how to make money decisions together. Plus, you will actually get some of your money tasks completed.

After working with thousands of couples, I know that this weekly money meeting is the most important commitment you can make. It will have a powerful effect on your money life because you are building trust—week after week after week. You are creating a place where you actually learn new money skills together, get your money tasks completed and develop more effective decision-making skills together. By giving yourselves a place to practice new money skills—and having the willingness and commitment to incorporate these skills into your life—you will change your money life. The weekly money meeting really works!

Exercise: Committing to a Weekly Money Meeting

On the same page as the previous commitment, write:

"I am willing to meet with my partner, _____, for a weekly money meeting. I will agree to schedule this meeting and make it happen, no matter what."

Now read this commitment statement to each other.

Before we move on to the third cornerstone of your new money structure—respect—let's list what does and does not happen in your weekly money meeting.

Here's what **does not** happen in this money meeting:

- This money meeting is **not** the time for talk about the children and their problems.

- It is **not** for talk about your in-laws or about your work or about what happened yesterday.

- If you are fighting, you will **not** continue the argument. You will put your fight aside and use the meeting to attend to your money life.

Being able to put aside these issues and others like them means you really are two adults in charge of your money life. You are two adults who have made a commitment.

Here's what **does** happen in the weekly money meeting:

- The money meeting is a scheduled, purposeful meeting to practice couple money communication and to make financial decisions as a couple.

- This money meeting is focused—there will be an agenda.

- It is frequent—you will meet weekly.

- It is time-limited—you will meet no more than one hour per week.

The only rule in your weekly money meeting is that you must treat each other with respect—the third cornerstone in your new money structure.

Respect: The Third Cornerstone

In chapter 6, I asked you to respect each other by not rolling your eyes or being otherwise distracted while listening to your partner. I'm now talking about a deeper form of respect that will anchor you as a couple—especially when you disagree. This respect is a very deep acceptance of each other.

When Jack said, "There's no reason for me to feel so alone and for Maria to feel so scared," it was a statement of deep respect—an acceptance of what both of them are feeling. Respect is very different from criticism and judgment. When criticizing or judging, you say things like, "*Why* are you feeling what you are feeling?" and "*What's the matter with you* that you are doing what you are doing?"

Showing respect means that you accept your partner for who he or she is. It doesn't mean you always agree with the feelings or the behaviors. It does means you see your partner as an intelligent, competent and caring person. It means you see your partner as the one you love and the one you don't want to lose.

> **Showing respect means that you accept your partner for who he or she is.**

A lack of respect for your partner is a component of most couples' money beliefs. Look again at your top three money beliefs. I would wager that at least one of them, and maybe all three, include the language of disrespect.

The kind of disrespect that couples feel and show each other is unique to personal partnerships. Think for a minute. Let's say you are in a business partnership. As business partners you have both invested money, time, dreams and energy into your business. As business partners, you have very different personalities. You both know that one of you is quite good at one aspect of the business, and the other is quite good at another aspect. You know that the differences in your skills and personalities are important to the balanced, successful management of your business.

What do you think would happen to your business if you treated each other with the same kind of disrespect that occurs in most personal partnerships? You know the answer. You would be out of business in short order. Neither one of you would tolerate the discounting, the sarcasm, the anger, the criticism and the judgment—the disrespect that many personal partners experience.

You also know that to run a successful business, you need to meet regularly with your business partner to discuss who is responsible for what and when and to review the overall direction of the business. This meeting time is particularly important *because* of your different skills and personalities.

How long do you think a business partnership would last if you never had business meetings? A business will not succeed—in the long run—if the partners don't treat each other with respect and meet regularly to discuss their business. These meetings symbolize that the partners are in charge of their business. Partners who wait for a crisis before meeting usually don't have a successful, stable business. These types of business partners don't know how to communicate or to plan for the future of their company.

Now, as personal partners, you have made a commitment to create a new money partnership. You will not be able to keep this commitment without meeting regularly and treating each other with respect. For those of you who cannot remember what respect feels like, here are the kinds of statements that reflect a feeling of respect:

- "I value you even when we disagree."
- "I'll treat you like I wish you would treat me."
- "I appreciate you even when you aren't as good as I am at a specific task."
- "Even though we are very different people, it is partly because of our differences that I fell in love with you."
- "Even though I don't always understand you and you don't always understand me, I value you and our relationship. I am absolutely committed to making our money partnership work."

Compromise: The Fourth Cornerstone

It's now time to actually schedule your weekly money meeting. Scheduling this meeting adds the fourth cornerstone to your new money structure: compromise.

Yes! The fourth cornerstone is the skill of compromise. Scheduling your weekly money meeting is only the beginning of practicing the skill of compromise. You will have many opportunities to practice this essential skill as you continue working through this book.

There are many phrases that describe compromise: reconcile our differences, mediate our differences, accommodate, create an understanding, create an alliance, form a synergistic relationship. I use the word *compromise* because for most people, compromise means some kind of giving up or loss. Use of the word *compromise* forces most couples to face their fears about loss in their relationships. Most couples have a fear of loss that sounds something like, "If you get yours, then I won't get mine." This statement reflects a basic belief in our society about scarcity. It's a belief that says, "There's not a way for both of us to feel satisfied. There's not a way for both of us to get what we need. One of us is going to lose."

The word *compromise* seems to trigger a fear in many men and women that there isn't enough—of anything—to meet both of their needs: if he gets more personal money, she will get less; if she goes to lunch with friends, he will get stuck with the kids; if she watches the news, he will have to do the dishes; if he gets home late, she will have to cook dinner again; and on and on. If this sounds familiar, maybe for you, like most people, compromise means losing something.

Be careful not to start intellectualizing here. By this I

mean your brain is saying things like, "Oh no, Ruth. I know this can be a win-win situation. Of course, she will have to agree to do the right thing here—then we can make it a win-win situation."

Or, your intellectualizing might sound like this: "Well, Ruth, I think it's important to be willing to give up what I want in order to make the family work. I just wish he felt the same way instead of just taking, taking, taking."

If you intellectualize the word *compromise*, you'll make a statement that sounds very mature and very proper. Then you'll add the second part of the statement, which takes a jab at your partner. I call this a politically correct way to blame your partner. And as you have already learned, blaming doesn't work.

The word *compromise* must be responded to on an emotional level, not an intellectual level. The word may trigger an emotional response that stops you from developing your new money skills as a couple. The word may trigger one of your beliefs, such as these beliefs in scarcity: "If you get yours, I won't get mine" or "He always wants too much" or "I always want too much" or "There's never enough money—ever" or "There's never enough time—ever."

The word *compromise* challenges these beliefs. It says that you have to find a way for both of you to get what you need. Compromise means stretching, not losing.

Compromise is not a sign of weakness but rather a sign of strength and confidence. Compromise asks you to see how far you can stretch toward your partner without losing yourself. These two qualities of compromise—stretching and not losing yourself—are essential to building this skill.

> **Compromise asks you to see how far you can stretch toward your partner without losing yourself.**

Compromise, just like any stretching, can be uncomfortable, especially if you haven't done it in a while. You must know that you are not truly losing yourself or what truly matters to you. And you must be willing to stretch—to give—toward your partner and what your partner needs.

Remember, compromise is not about loss. It's about creating a truly win-win situation. You are taking care of yourself while you are also helping your partner get what he or she needs. You are practicing the skill of compromise, which is a skill of partnership.

As a couple, you will need to practice the skill of compromise when scheduling your first weekly money meeting. You both will have to stretch your schedules to find the time to meet. You know that you have compromised when the time you pick may be slightly inconvenient for both of you. Compromise will feel a bit uncomfortable because you are stretching to accommodate your partner. You want your partner to know you are committed to stretching—committed to compromise.

Exercise: Scheduling Your First Weekly Money Meeting

Schedule your first weekly money meeting by following these steps:

1. Decide *when* you will meet and write this date down in your notebooks. If possible, schedule your meeting at the same time each week to help form a habit of meeting. Make this happen, even if you have to schedule a weekly baby-sitter. Be sure to write this time and day in your personal calendar. If someone asks you to do something at that time, say that you have a "business meeting" scheduled and can't make it. If, because of variability in your work schedules, you are not able to meet at the same time each week, then the *first* agenda item at each meeting will be to set the time for your next meeting.

2. Write down in your notebooks and in your calendars *where* you will meet.

3. Write down *how long* the money meeting will last. I recommend no more than one hour. As in other exercises, use a timer. It's easier for couples to wrap up their meeting if the timer indicates it's over rather than one of you saying it's over. If you need more than one hour, schedule a second meeting during the week.

4. Agree that the *agenda* for your weekly money meeting will be set by this book. (An agenda for this first meeting follows this chapter.)

5. Write in your notebooks a statement to yourself and your partner that affirms your commitment to *practicing respect* together. For example, "I will practice treating you as I wish you would treat me," or "Even though we are very different from each other, I value you and appreciate you. I will show you this through my actions and my words" or "No matter what, I will be nice!"

6. Read your statements to each other. These statements are your *new* money beliefs. How about that! You just formed new language—new beliefs that you are beginning to practice. You are changing!

Making Your Weekly Money Meeting Work

As you completed this exercise, you may have wondered why I asked you to decide where you will meet and for how long, as well as agree to a meeting agenda. As Julie and David demonstrate, some couples get stuck if they don't make these agreements:

"This won't work for us," Julie begins. "It really won't. We've set times to meet and nothing ever happens. In fact, it's made our marriage even worse."

The intensity in Julie's voice increases. "I have always kept any meeting we've set. I show up and wait, but when David doesn't show up, I go do something else. And I'm steaming. When he comes home, I ask where he was and guess what? He gets mad at me! He says things like, 'I'm trying to make this business work' or 'My meeting ran over' or 'What meeting? I didn't know we were going to meet today.' It's not worth it, Ruth. It'll never work for us."

I look at David and ask him what he remembers about past meetings with Julie.

"You know, Ruth, she's probably right." David doesn't look at Julie as he continues. "In the past I would agree to discuss something with Julie when *she* wanted to have the discussion."

Julie moves forward in her chair and starts to interrupt. David shakes his head and says, "Let me finish, Julie. I'm not blaming you. I know I used to, but I've learned a lot since we started working with Ruth. I get that it's not your fault."

Julie sits back as he continues, "I agree to the meetings and to the times, hoping I can make it. But I never write them down, and to tell the truth, I probably didn't want to meet with you. I knew you would be angry if I didn't show, but you would also be angry if I did and the meeting would just go on and on. So, I just conveniently forgot. She's right, Ruth. My track record isn't good."

I ask David if he feels differently about scheduling a meeting now—with a time frame and an agenda. He says he does. I ask if he understands that by keeping the commitment to meet, he is teaching *himself* that he is trustworthy, and he is teaching his wife that he can be trusted.

"That's what I really want," says David as he looks at Julie. "I want you to be able to trust me. I really do. But I need to be careful when I agree to meet with you. We may have to meet at odd times in order for me to be home on time. Are you willing to talk about the time?"

Before Julie answers, I ask if she would make a commitment to David to hold to the time frame and the agenda during their meetings. Julie needs to make sure David can trust her about the length and content of the meeting, just as David needs to keep his agreement to be home on time to meet.

"I understand," Julie explains quietly. "In the past, when I would finally get his attention, I think I tried to tell him everything all at once. I'm not blaming you either, David. I'm willing to keep to the agenda and the time. And I'm not sure what you mean by odd hours, but I'm willing to compromise about when we meet."

So, just like Julie and David, make sure to set a time to meet that works for both of you—no matter what. Keeping this commitment will help you build trust.

The issue of *where* to meet may seem obvious, but as Denise and Ted show us, this is not the case:

"We never met for our meeting," Denise tells me, clipping her words.

Ted interrupts and says, in the same angry tone, "That's because she never came to the study to meet."

"But I thought we would meet at the desk in the den!" Denise exclaims.

I listen a while longer to Ted and Denise debate whether their meeting should have been in the den or the study and then ask, "How big is the house you two live in? If you both really made a commitment to meet, couldn't one of you have hollered, 'Where are you?' and waited for an answer?"

Denise and Ted both grin involuntarily at the absurdity of the situation. Here we have two adults in their separate rooms waiting for the other, each obviously blaming the other.

So, make sure to decide *where* you will meet so you will be sure to find each other. Most couples meet at home because of the convenience. But if that doesn't work, get creative and find another place.

When Jack told me that the reason he missed a couple of meetings was because Maria was always hysterical and nothing got done anyway—which Maria, of course, denied—I suggested they meet at home and tape it. Then after the meeting, I asked them to sit quietly and listen to the tape. When the tape was over, they each had to name something they did that was useful to the meeting and something that was not useful. Then the meeting was over. Their meetings took longer, but they began to speak more respectfully. They both agreed that having to listen to their rudeness played back on tape was embarrassing. They started to speak more respectfully to each other, and they started to meet consistently. Because of this consistency, they started building trust.

Kim and Denny had trouble meeting because they also had difficulty holding the cornerstone of respect. Or as Kim put it, "Denny and I have a problem with being loud and mean." I suggested they get a baby-sitter and meet in the public library. They took turns taking notes on what decisions they made and who was supposed to do what. It worked. Being out in public—in a place where they would have been embarrassed to be loud and mean—helped them keep their commitment, helped them practice respect and helped them start to build trust.

Remember:

- Meeting consistently—week after week—will help you anchor your new money structure with trust.

- Working with each other—week after week—will help you learn the skill of compromise.

- Acting in a way that values your partner—meeting after meeting—will help you anchor your money life with respect.

Exercise: Making the Commitment

Before you finish today, complete this sentence in your notebooks:

"I agree to meet for our first official money meeting on _____ (day) at _____ (time) at _____ (place)." Remember to bring your notebooks to this meeting.

The agenda for your first weekly money meeting follows this chapter. Good luck!

Money Meeting #1

Welcome to your first official money meeting. As you learned in chapter 7, this weekly money meeting is a *symbol* that you are committed to changing your money life as a couple and it is a *place* to practice the couple communication and decision-making skills you are learning in this book.

For this meeting, the agenda is set for you. As you continue through this book, you will practice developing an agenda yourself so that these money meetings become an ongoing part of your money life as a couple.

Money Meeting Agenda

1. Confirm or decide when, where and at what time you will hold your money meeting next week. Write it down—both of you—in your notebooks and in your personal calendars—in ink.

2. Remind yourselves that you have signed an agreement to practice the four anchoring cornerstones of your new money structure: commitment, trust, respect and compromise.

3. The agenda for the rest of this meeting is to work through chapter 8 together.

Eight

This Isn't How I'd Spend Money If I Were Single

H ow do we get started on a budget, Ruth?" Diane asks.

"We write out all the numbers on paper," says Will, "but it never works. Something always takes the money that was supposed to be for something else." Will sounds discouraged. "We just never seem to be able to get started."

Most couples have difficulty forming a budget because they start at the *end* of the budgeting process rather than at the beginning. It's like learning to read by starting with Tolstoy's *War and Peace* rather than a basic reader. Can you imagine? Very few people would have ever learned to read if their beginning reader text was *War and Peace*.

To form a budget successfully, it is necessary to start with a practice budget to hone your skills. This process of practicing a system of budgeting must be as simple as a beginning reader.

This simple practice system asks you to do three things:

1. Practice working together as a couple.
2. Learn to reach an agreement on the budgeted numbers.
3. Learn to stay within an agreed amount of money.

Practice Working Together as a Couple

You already know how different you two are. And, you are actually here—sitting together—at your first official money meeting. Before you try to form a complete, complicated budget, you need to practice working together with money itself.

Remember, you can't learn to read by starting with Tolstoy. You have to be willing to begin at the beginning. Working together successfully doesn't just happen. Learning to work together involves building a new skill base and showing respect for each other with every decision made. The motto here is, *Be nice!* When you feel a sarcastic comment coming on—bite your tongue and be nice! Then, in a kind, respectful manner, talk together.

If you feel your partner is discounting what you say or not affirming you, hold back the harsh comment and *nicely* and *respectfully* explain what you just heard and how it made you feel. Being nice doesn't mean acquiescing to your partner. As you learned in chapter 2, acquiescing is a response that doesn't work in the long run.

Being nice means that you show respect even when you

don't agree with each other. It means that you speak to each other in a manner that respects you, individually, and respects your partner.

Learn to Reach an Agreement on the Budgeted Numbers

To reach an agreement on the budgeted numbers, you need to consciously use all four of the cornerstones of your new money structure: commitment, trust, respect and compromise. And, oh, what an opportunity you will have in this chapter to use the fourth cornerstone of compromise!

In chapter 7, you learned that instead of an "If you get yours, I won't get mine" attitude, which reflects our fear of loss, compromise sounds like this:

- "*How* do you get yours *while* I get mine?"
- "How do *we* get *ours?*"
- "Where are *we* willing to *stretch* to make changes in *our* budget that really work?
- "How are *we* going to make *our* budget work?"

This is the language of creative compromise. This is a skill that you as a couple have to learn, because without it, you won't be able to budget successfully—not even with this practice budget.

Learn to Stay Within an Agreed Amount of Money

You probably thought that if you could actually agree on the numbers, your budget was complete. Wrong! This third part of our practice system is necessary for a budget to really work.

Otherwise, you simply have created a balance sheet. It is common for couples to mistake a balance sheet for a budget.

A balance sheet records what you *did* financially. A budget is a financial action plan that tells you what you are going to *do*. The data on a balance sheet is history. If your balance sheet shows you have overspent, it's too late to do anything about it. With a budget, you purposefully plan so your life today and tomorrow works—so you stay with what you planned and your money plan is successful.

> **A balance sheet records what you *did* financially. A budget is a financial action plan that tells you what you are going to *do*.**

A practice budget helps you learn to work together as a couple, reach an agreement on the budgeted numbers and stay within the agreed amount of money.

Are you ready?

Setting Up a Practice Budget

To begin practicing, we'll take just a small part of the total budget. The part you will use to practice is the weekly flexible part of the budget. When we think of things that break a budget, we usually think of major expenses such as car repairs, life insurance premiums you forgot about, an emergency visit by the plumber or an unexpected trip to the dentist. These are reasons most people think their budgets fail. But studies show that this isn't why budgets fail.

Budgets that are so *carefully* calculated fail because money seems to disappear from your checkbook. Right? In your mind you remember how much is supposed to be there, but now it isn't. What happened?

Life happened. Day-to-day living costs drain money out of your checkbook. These costs turn your checkbook into a *money sieve*, and these small expenses quickly add up to a large amount of money. For example, you write a check for gas. You stop to pick up milk and a few other necessities. You get your hair cut. You pick up the dry cleaning and laundry. You stop to pick up a pizza for the family on a busy night. You stop at the cash machine more times than you remember.

These are the real budget busters. This money sieve causes two problems. First, there is an ongoing leak of money out of your checkbook, and when it's time to pay the bills, the money isn't there to pay them. And second, the money sieve causes stress—both personally and as a couple. This stress usually causes blaming. You ask yourself or your partner, "Where did all the money go?" You have no answer. You have nothing to show for all that money.

It is these kinds of flexible weekly expenses that you will use to practice budgeting. If you are willing to make the practice budget work, you will be able to solve these two problems of a money sieve. You will be able to protect the money in your checkbook from these small, but essential, daily and weekly expenses. And in the process you will reduce the stress caused by the money sieve.

This practice budget doesn't ask you to plan how you will pay the car repair bill this month. That would be asking you to start the budgeting process with Tolstoy. Trust me. We will get to Tolstoy and we will get to the car repair. But by then, you will have the skills you need to successfully manage a complete budget together.

For now, you will decide together how much money you need to budget for your flexible weekly expenses. Use the following four steps to set up your practice budget.

Step 1: Make a List and Check It Twice

Make a list of your weekly expenses as a couple:

- groceries, eating out and convenience foods;
- entertainment and small gifts such as for children's parties or a friend's birthday;
- gas, children's allowances, drug store items and household items such as toilet paper, shampoo, pet food and school fees;
- money for you and your partner to use at your own discretion, such as for lunches, newspapers, haircuts and parking fees.

Make a list and check it twice—both of you! Have you forgotten anything?

Step 2: Determine What You Currently Spend

Write down how much money you spend weekly for each of these expenses. The important word here is *weekly*. If you're not sure how much you spend, guess. Don't forget—if you disagree on the amount, *be nice and compromise!*

Will and Diane, who we heard from at the start of this chapter, are having trouble here:

"Be nice!" Will explodes. "Yeah, right. Do you know how much she wants to spend on groceries and the kids each week? $400! We can't afford $400! And you tell me to be nice?!"

"I'll tell you what," Will continues, "this isn't how I'd spend money if I were single!"

"See, Ruth," Diane explains, "every time we start talking about what our life costs us, he gets mad because he doesn't want to hear it! He makes some crack about being single."

Diane turns to Will, "Well, you're not single, and that's what we're spending. Pull your head out of the sand and get real!"

Diane raises a valid point. Looking at the numbers can be scary, and when some people get scared, they get angry. Others get sad. So instead of getting angry or sad, get to work, together, building a budget for your weekly flexible expenses. While you're working, don't forget about respect. Remember, you are practicing commitment, trust, respect and, the big one, *compromise*.

So write down the amount of money you both believe needs to be budgeted for these weekly flexible expenses. I'm asking you to use weekly figures because you will be meeting weekly for your money meetings. If you "bust your budget," your next weekly meeting is just a few days away.

Step 3: Practice Using Cash

This practice budget involves using cash—actual paper bills and real coins—for all of your weekly flexible expenses.

"Cash!" says Will. "If we use cash, I'll never know where the money went. At least with checks I have some idea what's costing so much."

"Oh yes," Diane agrees. "When I have cash, it just seems to disappear."

Diane and Will's method of budgeting has not worked. So they, like you, need to try something different. You need a whole new model for budgeting because the old way isn't working—that's why you're reading this book! You and your partner have decided to learn a new way of working together in your money life.

So try a new way. Be willing to use cash as a learning tool. Inherent in this method of using cash itself are the two standards of budgeting that are essential for a budget to work:

1. **The budget must have absolute stopping places for spending.** To make your budget work, you have to know when you have reached your limit. And when you reach this limit, you have to stop spending. If you budget $25 for drugstore items and then go to the store and buy $32 worth of items, you will probably ignore the overrun if you are writing a check. If you are using a credit card, you probably wouldn't even realize you are $7 over your budget. However, if you are using cash and you have only $25 to spend, you'll stop. You have to stop. The budget just worked!

2. **You must know how much you can spend *while* you are actually spending the money.** *While* you are grocery shopping, you have to know how much you have to spend *and* force yourself not to spend any more than that amount of money. Remember, you are creating a budget, not a balance sheet. As you have already learned, a balance sheet is about what you have already done and can't change. A budget is an action plan that works.

For Will and Diane, their balance sheet—which they keep on their computer—usually comes up in deficit.

"You're right," Will says. "Every time I add up the checks, I say, 'We're *way* over again. What happened?'" He adds, looking at his wife, "Then I say to Diane, 'You've got to stop spending.'"

"Ruth," says Diane, "he isn't nice, like he says he is, when he gets mad."

"You're right," Will responds, "but I get so frustrated because we can never seem to get through a month without going over."

"And," Diane adds, "the really hard part is there's nothing we can do about it. And then we're really in trouble because we start the next month behind."

Here we are just practicing, but any budget won't work unless these two standards are followed. So remember, (1) the budget must have absolute stopping places for spending, and (2) you must know how much you can spend *while* you are actually spending the money.

In our society, there are four general ways to work with money: savings accounts, checking accounts, credit cards and cash. Of these, cash is the only tool that implicitly holds these two standards of budgeting.

Cash is the only money tool that implicitly holds the two standards of budgeting.

When you use a checkbook, you are simply guessing what you have to spend on a certain item. You write a check for groceries, knowing that the car insurance and the child care have to somehow come out of the same balance.

The same happens with a savings account, with one added problem. You may not even know what the balance is in the account.

Most people don't have any idea how much they have charged on their credit cards until they get their monthly bill. A budget won't work using credit cards because there is no natural stopping place—no set limit. The credit card bill does work as an effective balance sheet—it tells you what you spent this month. But you are not developing a balance sheet in this chapter, you are developing the skills of budgeting.

Cash is the only money tool that *implicitly* allows you to successfully practice the two basic standards of budgeting.

Step 4: Set Up the Logistics for Your Cash Budget

You have already decided how much money you need each week for the weekly flexible expenses. Now you have to figure out how to make your cash budget actually work.

Take your time working out the logistics of a cash budget. Learning to make it work is a big part of learning to budget.

Who will go to the bank or the cash machine and withdraw the cash each week? This means that your budgeted amount of weekly cash (from step 2) needs to be physically taken out of the bank each week.

Which day of the week will this cash be taken out of the bank? In other words, which day is cash payday? I recommend that you make this the same day as your weekly money meeting. That would be today, then, since this is your money meeting.

During the week, where will the cash be kept and by whom? Decide what items on your cash list are individual personal expenditures and what items are for the two of you and your family. For example, haircuts for each of you are probably part of your personal money, and haircuts for your young children are family money. Lunches out when you are apart are personal money, but eating out as a couple or a family comes from family money. Your lists may look something like this:

This Week's Cash Budget

Yours	Mine	Ours
Haircut $_____	Haircut $_____	Kids' haircuts $_____
Lunches $_____	Lunches $_____	Eating out $_____
Personal stuff	Personal stuff	Household stuff
$_____	$_____	$_____
Magazines/books	Magazines/books	Small gifts
$_____	$_____	$_____
Clothes $_____	Clothes $_____	Kids' clothes $_____
Toys $_____	Toys $_____	Kids' toys $_____
		Groceries $_____
		Family entertainment
		$_____

Totals for the Week

Yours $_____	Mine $_____	Ours $_____

Each of you will keep your personal cash in your wallets or wherever you want, but you need to decide where the household cash will be kept. I recommend that you keep the household cash in separate categories—for example, grocery money in a separate wallet or envelope. This system works for couples as they start practicing budgeting because it gives them a basis for evaluating if they have budgeted the correct amount for each category. If the grocery money envelope is empty just a few days into the week, then that budgeted amount may need to be adjusted at the next meeting. Without separate categories, you will run out of money and not know which budgeted item is causing the shortage. Then, if you're like many couples, you will quit because you get discouraged.

Most couples find that if you divide the cash into as many categories as you have listed in your practice budget—and put the money for each category in a separate wallet or envelope— the budget works better.

And, as part of your commitment to each other, don't steal from one envelope to pay for something in another category. When a particular budget category is out of money, you have to stop. Don't spend any more money in that budget category until you put more money into it at the next cash payday. If you believe the reason the category ran out of money is because you miscalculated, adjust the budget amount at the next meeting, not before.

When the money is gone, you stop spending. The cash is simply a boundary that tells you when to stop spending so you can keep your commitment to your partner.

Don't panic! If you run out of grocery money before the end of the week, you won't starve. You will be uncomfortable—because you are stretching to get your needs met within a specific amount of money. Remember, stretching is compromise, and compromise can be uncomfortable.

If this stretching feels more than just uncomfortable—if you really are scared or panicked—you have just stumbled over one of your money beliefs. You know you have stumbled over a money belief if your emotional response is greater than what is actually happening. If you are scared that you will run out of grocery money or won't have enough to buy lunches, stop! You know you have enough food in the kitchen. No one is going to starve this week. Come on! If you run out of lunch money, there's something in the kitchen you can take to work to eat—you won't starve. Right? It isn't the budget that is causing you to panic. Your panic is coming from your beliefs, which are causing a bigger negative emotional response than what this cash budget deserves.

> **You know you have stumbled over a money belief if your emotional response is greater than what is actually happening.**

Kate experienced just this situation:

"As I looked at the menu in the restaurant," Kate says, "I realized I didn't have enough money to order my favorite salad. I wanted to scream! I thought, 'I work hard. I make a lot of money. And I can't even order a salad?' I was furious, Ruth, at you, for telling us to do this stupid exercise. I was furious with myself for agreeing to it.

"Then I looked up from the menu," Kate continues, "and my colleague was looking at me strangely. She asked if I was all right. I knew I needed to pull myself together. I told her I was fine and ordered a bowl of soup and a croissant. Actually it was delicious.

"Later," says Kate, "when I was back in my office, I thought about the anger—almost rage—that I felt over a silly salad! I remembered what you said about beliefs. One of my beliefs is, 'There's never enough—ever.' When I was a kid there wasn't enough food or clothes. My rage wasn't at you, Ruth, or about the salad. I just got scared that I couldn't get what I wanted.

I felt like a child again. Incredible!"

Kate's voice is stronger as she continues. "I made a commitment to continue the weekly cash. I need to teach myself that even if we're on a budget, there's enough money. I have nothing to be scared of."

Do you see how Kate first identified where she got stuck and then reworded her belief? This is a belief and behavior change!

Again, if during this practice time your emotional response seems greater than the situation calls for, stop! Ask yourself, What am I feeling right now? Is my feeling connected to one of my beliefs? How can I change the language of my belief so it gives me emotional and financial freedom—so I don't feel scared or angry and can keep my budgeting commitment to myself and my partner?

Neil and Anne are also working out the logistics of a cash budget:

"Well, Ruth, I'm still using the silly cash like I said I would." Neil is looking at me with a grin.

"He wasn't smiling a few days ago," Anne interjects.

"She's right, Ruth," Neil continues. "I really had trouble keeping to the agreement. I earn a lot of money each year, and here I am like a kid with an allowance. But I did it because I said I would."

Neil's grin widens as he continues, "I was afraid my business partners would make fun of me, but instead I've turned into a kind of role model. And they don't even know what I'm doing! At a business lunch I took out a $100 bill instead of my credit card, like I always do. It was the beginning of the week, after all, and I still had a $100 bill. My partners thought I was showing off! They didn't think I was a kid on an allowance, they just saw me pay with a large bill. It was great."

He continues, "Just a couple of days ago, we went to lunch again. I only had a few dollars left, so I ordered soup and a salad and told them I was ordering light as part of my work-out routine." Neil chuckled. "They acted embarrassed at their food choices. I couldn't believe it! But Anne will tell you I wasn't happy this week with this silly cash."

Anne nods her head vigorously.

"But I made it!" Neil says, pleased with himself. "If this is what it takes to make this money work, and if Anne and I can negotiate a slight raise in this silly cash, I can do this. It's hard to not have money right at my fingertips for whatever I want—like with my credit card—but I can do this. In fact, I like the idea of starting a new trend at the office."

You can do this too. So try stretching. You can survive for one week, no matter what happens.

Will you keep track of the cash so you know how it is spent? My advice is to *not* keep track of anything more than you need to. Will and Diane found this advice helpful:

"Oh, I know how I can do this," Will visibly brightens. "Instead of having all these programs listed separately on the computer, I can combine them all under weekly cash."

Diane interrupts, "At least this way, your computer sheets and our actual budget might match—and maybe you won't be so angry all the time."

Now that you have planned *how* you will set up your practice budget using cash, begin today, if possible, so you have a full week to practice before your next weekly money meeting.

Before you are finished with your money meeting, make sure you review when, where and what time you will meet

again. At your next money meeting, use the agenda that follows this chapter.

Have fun this week with your cash. I know you will both
learn a lot.

Money Meeting #2

☞

Welcome to your second weekly money meeting. Congratulations on *twice* keeping your commitment to meet for an official money meeting. You know now that you need an ongoing time to practice building your communication and decision-making skills.

Money Meeting Agenda

1. Confirm where and at what time you will hold your money meeting next week. As you did last week, write the date and time in your notebooks and personal calendars—in ink.

2. Evaluate the cash budget that you worked with this week by answering these questions:

   - Did you keep your commitment to use cash only this week? If so, what happened that you are especially pleased about?

   - If you didn't keep your commitment, why not? What allowed you to decide to break your commitment—to break the trust with your partner?

   - What will you do next time to keep your commitment—to keep the trust?

   - What did you learn concerning the amount of money available for you to spend? Was it enough? Was it too much? If it wasn't enough, what expenses/costs did you underestimate when calculating the amount you would need?

- How much do you think you will need to make cash budgeting work?

- What did you learn about the amount of money you had available *as a couple* to spend? Which categories have leftover money in them?

It's all right to have leftover money—in fact it's a good sign. Most people never spend exactly the same amount of money each week on groceries, for example. If this week was low at the grocery store, next week may be higher. And most people don't get their hair cut each week, so you want to save that money until it is time for a haircut.

Like you, Diane and Will are discovering how to work with cash:

"So you mean," Diane says, "if I don't spend all the grocery money each week or my personal money, I don't get less the next week?"

"Right!" I answer.

"Will and I thought we would save money by using less cash this week."

"Diane," I explain, "if you do that, you're setting yourself up for exactly the same argument the two of you have now—Will says you spend more than you're supposed to.

"What if this week," I continue, "you have guests and need to spend more at the grocery store? Where will you get that extra cash? From the checkbook? You can't. That will break trust with Will."

"I get it," Will interrupts. "She saves money from one week to spend on a week that costs more. It's just like

I save my haircut money each week until I have to pay for it."

"But, Will," Diane says, "I'm not the only one who goes to the grocery store. You have to stay within the cash too when you make a trip to the store. And the wine we buy for entertaining has to come out of the grocery money."

"If that's true, Ruth, then we're going to need more money in the grocery envelope," Will says.

"See," Diane says, her voice almost gleeful. "I'm not always the one who says we need more money."

Will chuckles and concedes the point.

- Do you need to make any adjustments, like Will and Diane, in your amounts of cash as you begin a new week?

- What did you each learn about yourself and your money beliefs by working with cash this past week? Which of your money beliefs affected your individual spending decisions? What was the effect? Remember, if an emotional response was greater than seemed appropriate, you simply stumbled over an old belief. Did it seem like "There's never enough money" or "I never get mine" or "I shouldn't have to do this" or "I don't want to do this" or "This is way too hard, I can't do this"? So again, what beliefs affected your spending decisions this week?

- If your beliefs made it hard to keep your commitment this past week, what will you say to yourself next week to help you keep your commitment? For

example, your new language—your new beliefs—
may sound like this: "I *do* have to do this. I have to
learn for myself and for my partner that I can do
this—we can do this—we have to do this—to make
our money life work" or "I'm not alone—we're
working together" or "Even though this work is
hard, we can do this—we have done harder things"
or "I deserve to have a money life that works—my
partner deserves it and our family deserves it."

• What will you *do* individually and together to make
the cash work next week? Yes, I want you to practice for another week.

Remember, all the skills you will need to make a "real
budget" work are contained in this practice cash budget.
You need to practice—week after week—so when you
put together a real budget (in chapters 10, 11 and 13), it
will work for you. As you already know, a budget is more
than a list of expenses. To make a budget work, you need
to develop the skills of commitment, respect, trust and
compromise. Decide what you will do individually and
together to make the cash practice budget work so you
can continue learning and building this new model.

Will and Diane have made their own decisions:

"I know what I have to do this week," says Will. "I
can't carry my credit card. I took it out a couple of times
this week without even thinking. Both times I actually
had enough money on me, but I just didn't want to spend
it. So I used my card."

"So that's why you have personal money left over!"
Diane interrupts. "And you were gloating that you had

some left and I ran out! Now I know why. But I'll make you a deal. If you leave your credit card at home, I'll leave the checkbook at home. I used it twice at the grocery story when I didn't have enough cash. Grocery shopping is going to be harder—but I'll do it."

"Okay," says Will. "We have a deal. Should be an interesting week!"

Diane and Will just made an agreement that will help them keep their commitment to spend within their cash budget. They are keeping their commitment to make the cash budget work.

When you have decided what you need to do—individually and as a couple—to really make the cash budget work this week, make an agreement and write it in your notebooks.

3. You have done well working within the agenda for this money meeting. Now, go ahead and begin working through chapter 9 together.

Nine

Creating a Road Map
for Your Life

Just think what you have done so far, together!

- You have explored your childhood money history—your earliest money training.

- You have identified the emotional conclusions you formed from that history—your money beliefs.

- You connected the effects of those money beliefs to your specific money behaviors—behaviors that may have been affecting your spending, your earning and/or your saving as an adult.

- You have begun to change both your money beliefs and your money behaviors.

Throughout this process, you learned to communicate respectfully as you shared information with your partner. Then you took your communication one step further and identified how your individual beliefs and corresponding behaviors were compounded by your partner's beliefs and behaviors, creating estrangement, misunderstanding, confusion, hopelessness, frustration, anger or simply benign neglect in your money life. You felt stuck—together.

Many couples feel like they are working harder but have less. They are earning more money but seem to have less to work with after paying basic family expenses.

"That's me," says Will. "I'm working more hours—sometimes even weekends—and it's not enough. Then Diane and the kids are upset because I'm not home enough. Every month—I mean every single month, Ruth—I think, 'If we can just get through this month, then maybe something will change.'"

"Do you know what I do each month?" Diane says in a small voice. "I'm a little embarrassed about this, but it gets me through the month. I think about winning the lottery. I actually plan—first we'd put away college money, then we'd put an addition on the house, then we'd all go on a wonderfully expensive vacation. Maybe to Australia, where we'd swim with the dolphins."

I watch Will roll his eyes as his wife talks. Diane sees it, too.

"Will," Diane's voice is much stronger now, "give me a break! This is the only way I can get through each month without giving up. I feel so stuck! And," she continues, "if you told the truth, Will, you know you fantasize, too. I've heard you."

Will grins involuntarily in agreement.

When we can't stand feeling stuck and discouraged, many of us fantasize. "If I won the lottery," "if I wrote a bestselling novel," "if I earned twice as much" and "if a long-lost uncle died and left me all his money" are all dreams that both men and women have. These dreams come out of the frustration of feeling stuck and not knowing what to do about it. These dreams come out of trying to feel some emotional respite from the hopelessness of feeling stuck. Most men and women swing from one emotional extreme to the other—from feeling stuck and hopeless to fantasizing and dreaming.

> **Most men and women swing from one emotional extreme to the other—from feeling stuck and hopeless to fantasizing and dreaming.**

There's nothing wrong with fantasizing. Sometimes it's a wonderful respite from feeling stuck. The danger with fantasizing is that it may stop you from creating solutions to your real-life problems. Dreams may be substitutes for purposeful living—for creating solutions, for planning and for setting goals.

The difference between dreaming and setting goals is simply the difference between *wishing*—which is the dream—and *creating*—which is the goal. It's the difference between hoping and planning. The difference between dreams and goals is the difference between *wanting* something to happen and *causing* something to happen.

> **The difference between dreams and goals is the difference between *wanting* something to happen and *causing* something to happen.**

There's nothing wrong with dreaming unless you get stuck there. Dreaming is always the beginning of setting goals. Goals make wishes happen. Setting goals is about deciding to do something or be something or have something and then planning to make it happen.

The Consequences of Not Setting Goals

Staying stuck in dreaming and not setting clear, purposeful goals can have three major consequences. The first consequence is that as a couple, *you may find yourselves heading in two different life directions and not know how to reconnect.* You may think you are saving so you can travel during your retirement and your partner may think you are saving to pay off the mortgage early. You may be expecting to buy a vacation home like your parents did and your partner is planning to start a new business.

"That's what happened to us," Maria interjects. "We worked so hard to save money, I thought it would mean an early retirement for both of us so we could travel and have fun together. I didn't know Jack was planning to take the money and start his own business."

"That's not fair," Jack says forcefully. "I told you year after year that I wanted to start my own business. I told you. I really did."

"But, Jack, I never took that seriously," says Maria. "I thought you were dreaming, just like my dream to buy a house on the lake. I know I'll never get a house there. I never knew you were really going to take the money for your business."

Setting goals as a couple creates a mutually agreed-upon map for your life together. Goals connect you and your partner so you can create a life that both of you want.

> **Setting goals as a couple creates a mutually agreed-upon map for your life together.**

The second consequence of staying stuck in dreaming and not setting clear, purposeful goals is *having to learn to live with regrets*. One of the most frequent statements I hear from older clients is, "I always thought I would . . . start my own business . . . travel . . . invest . . . have a family. . . ." These statements are always said with deep sadness.

Couples in the process of creating change in their money lives often find the regret stage of the process to be difficult. Every change—large or small—has a place where you say to each other, "If only we had known how to do this earlier" or "If only we had started saving money when we were first married" or "If only we. . . ." This "if only" stage is a normal part of the process of change. You need to be willing to go through this stage, without blaming each other.

This process doesn't involve learning to *live* with regrets. Living with regrets is a permanent emotional state. It is saying, "I've always wanted to do something but will never be able to do it." For most of us, this is a frustrating, hopeless, grief-ridden and stuck place. It's a place where blame thrives, and it's a state you don't want to be in—ever.

When men and women stay stuck in dreaming and don't learn how to set goals, they must learn to live with the regret of what might have been. Setting goals reduces regrets and can make dreams happen. Instead of living with regrets, it is a feeling of regret as a part of the process of change.

The third major consequence of not setting goals is that *your budget won't work*. Specific goals must be a part of planning your budget. This is why you will work with this step of setting goals now. In the next chapter, you will put all the components of your total budget together.

Goals have to be clearly stated to make your budget work. Quite simply, if your goals aren't part of your budget, they will remain dreams. Most goals involve money, to a greater or lesser degree. If your goals aren't part of your budget, they won't be funded. Your budget is the plan for how your money will be spent. When you set your goals, you are deciding how your money will be spent. Another way to say this is that the goal is the driver, and the budget is the vehicle. The goal drives the budget.

> **The goal is the driver, and the budget is the vehicle. The goal drives the budget.**

Without clear, conscious goals, your budget is simply a monthly survival vehicle. After a period of time, simply surviving becomes discouraging. Couples feel as if they are not getting ahead—and they're not.

Transforming Dreams into Goals

You can see how Will and Diane are struggling with this idea:

"So, you're saying I should budget for Australia?" asks Diane. "But if I put a trip to Australia into the budget, we wouldn't be able to pay all the bills—we'd run out of money. We can't afford luxuries like that."

What Diane is saying is that she and Will can't afford to turn their dreams into goals. I ask Will if going to Australia is a dream of his.

"Now, don't laugh," Will answers. "But I've always wanted to hold a koala bear." Diane smiles. "I want to see the outback. Diane and I watched a video on Australia at a friend's house and we both fell in love with the country. I just know, though, that it's an impossible dream. Say," he continues with a laugh, "isn't that a song?" They both laugh together.

This is the first time I have seen Will and Diane laugh together. I tell them that this is what goals can do for a couple. A couple can start dreaming together and then take that dream and put it into their budget. It is now a clear goal. It is going to happen—sometime.

At that, they both stop laughing. Will shakes his head and says, "Diane is right. We can't afford this Australia nonsense. We have to pay our bills."

I ask if they remember learning earlier in this book about the power of symbols. I suggest they get a jar and label it "Australia." I tell them to cut a slot in the lid of the jar to put coins and bills into and then glue the lid to the jar—so no one can pilfer any money.

I then suggest they create a new budgeting category in their practice cash budget. This category will be called "Australia." Maybe this category will get only $5 per week—for now. But their dream of Australia has been turned into a goal by deciding to "put their money where their dream is."

It may take awhile, but the jar is a symbol that says they will get to Australia. As Diane and Will get more and more control of their money life, they will be able to increase the amount and transfer it to a savings account named "Australia."

Transforming dreams into goals also creates a greater motivation to make your budget work, because now the budget isn't just about the monotony of monthly bills and expenses—it is also about dreams. It is about hope.

Diane agrees. "If I have money left over in the weekly cash, I could put some of it into the jar. I really could. I think I can figure out how to squeeze a little money each week into that jar."

Will simply grins at his wife.

Again, the hope and excitement that you hear in Will and Diane comes from transforming their dreams into goals. Nothing else has really changed in their money life. But they are feeling more hope than they have felt for awhile.

So, now it's time for you to work on developing clear goals from your dreams. There are four steps to make this transformation work. Do the first three steps *individually* and work on the final step *together*.

Step 1: Write down what you want to have, to do, to be, to see.

These are your hopes and dreams. Some will be just about you and some will include your partner. Don't worry about being practical. Fantasize! What do you want in your life? What do you want for the two of you?

Step 2: Create a time frame for these dreams and hopes.

Future date #1: Look at a calendar and write down the date that is exactly six months from today. This is an important first date because you will have to start working right now to make your six-month goal happen. How old will you be on that date? Write your age in your notebook.

Future date #2: Write down the date that is two years from today. How old will you be on that date? Write your age.

Future date #3: Write down the date that is five years from today. How old will you be on that date? Write your age.

Future date #4: Write down the date that is ten years from today. Write your age.

Future date #5: Think for a moment of an age that you consider to be "old age." Write that age in your notebook. On what date will you be that age? Write down that date.

Now, write these dates in your notebook linearly, starting with the six-month date. Leave space between the dates. It will look like this:

My Goal-Setting Chart

Date six months from now: _____

Date two years from now: _____

Date five years from now: _____

Date ten years from now: _____

Date when you are at "old age":   _____

Step 3: Fit your hopes and dreams from step 1 into the time frame you created in step 2.

Remember, you are still working individually in your notebook. Now, your paper will look like this:

My Goal-Setting Chart

	What do I want?
Date six months from now:	
Date two years from now:	
Date five years from now:	
Date ten years from now:	
Date when you are at "old age":	

Some of your goals will be very personal goals; some will be goals for you as a couple. Remember, do not limit yourself to strictly financial goals—all of your goals require money, to one degree or another, to make them happen.

Still working alone, add one more column across the top of your paper to finish step 3. The column should say, "What I will need to do *by this date* to make this goal happen." What you need to accomplish may involve money or may be specific, nonmoney tasks. Write down whatever you think needs to be done to get what you want.

My Goal-Setting Chart

	What do I want?	What I will do
Date six months from now:		
Date two years from now:		
Date five years from now:		
Date ten years from now:		
Date when you are at "old age":		

To make this step work, it may be helpful to work backwards on your chart. In other words, start setting goals by thinking about what you want your old age to be like. What choices do you want to make sure you have? Where do you want to live? With whom?

An older man once said, "If I had known I was going to live this long, I'd have taken better care of my teeth!" So, if you want to have good teeth when you are old, then make sure that every six months or so you "budget" both time and money for a dental visit—starting six months from now. Seriously, this is how the goal-setting chart works. If working backwards makes sense to you, then decide what you want for each time frame and write it down, moving closer and closer to your present age.

When you and your partner have both completed your charts, go to step 4.

Step 4: Work together to set goals.

Before you begin, recall the four cornerstones of your new money structure that you are practicing: commitment, trust, respect and compromise. You will need all four for this step, particularly respect and compromise.

Be sure to use a pencil with a very large eraser for this step. You are about to put together a puzzle called "Your Life." The puzzle pieces are each of your hopes and dreams and the time periods of your life. Your job is to make the pieces fit so you *both* feel hopeful about your future.

Remember, all couples have hopes, dreams, assumptions and expectations that are unspoken to each other. It is these unspoken assumptions that create problems. You may be assuming you have the same goals, but don't forget that you are each unique individuals with very different perspectives and very different dreams and hopes.

All couples have hopes, dreams, assumptions and expectations that are unspoken to each other. It is these unspoken assumptions that create problems.

To get started on the "Your Life" puzzle, take a large piece of paper. Together, make the same columns you made individually in step 3 on the same paper. This will be your chart for setting goals as a couple.

On this sheet of paper, you need to add more categories to the columns. It will look like the chart on page 148.

When you have complied the information from your individual sheets onto this one sheet, continue to step 5.

Step 5: For each time frame, discuss and then write down a couple strategy to make all three sets of goals work: yours, mine and ours.

Now the hard work begins. Again, don't forget the four cornerstones, especially respect and compromise. You will really get a chance to practice compromising in this step.

Is your eraser handy? You're going to need it. Remember, this is your life. Together, you have to make it work. You can do this. You are a committed, creative partnership.

Again, the task here is to come up with a strategy to make all three sets of goals work: yours, mine and ours.

Our Goal-Setting Chart

	What do I want?	What I will do	What I need to do
Date six months from now: *Yours:* *Mine:* *Ours:*			
Date two years from now: *Yours:* *Mine:* *Ours:*			
Date five years from now: *Yours:* *Mine:* *Ours:*			
Date ten years from now: *Yours:* *Mine:* *Ours:*			
Date when you are at "old age": *Yours:* *Mine:* *Ours:*			

- Where do you need to compromise your individual goals?
- How do you need to think differently about your lives?
- How will you make your goals, your partner's goals and your goals as a couple work in each time frame?

To be in a partnership for life, you need to find a way to make all three of these areas work, and you have to be willing to compromise. Compromise may involve timing. One of you may have to move a goal into a different time frame. Another part of compromising may involve changing the magnitude of the goal. Diane and Will's process illustrates this concept:

"Will, I know what we can do," says Diane. "We have our 'Australia' jar. Goodness knows how long that'll take—maybe twenty years. Why don't we go to Australia for our thirtieth wedding anniversary?"

They actually grin at each other, again. "But since Will loves to fish and the kids love to camp . . ."

Will interrupts, "You hate camping, Diane."

"I don't actually hate it," Diane contradicts. "I've always been so resentful because we couldn't have a 'nice' vacation. But, if we can borrow my parents' camper trailer—and I know we can—we can park it by a lake and actually take a vacation each year.

"See," Diane explains to me, "both Will and I have vacation as a goal starting this year and every year. We can go camping while we're stuffing our 'Australia' jar."

Like Will and Diane, you each have to be willing to make changes from what you assumed were the goals. In addition, you each need to take a stand on what is important to you personally. This is the art of the compromise—being willing to change and being willing to stand up for what is important.

> **This is the art of the compromise—being willing to change and being willing to stand up for what is important.**

This fifth step, discussing and then writing down a strategy to make all three sets of goals work, can be very difficult. And it is critical. If you aren't willing to make this step work, your partnership will not be successful in the long term. You will both feel too stuck, too frustrated and too hopeless.

Also, if you aren't willing to make this step work, the next chapter, which is about a budget, will not work. As you have already learned, a budget is simply a tool to make your lives happen—to realize your goals.

If you aren't clear about your goals, the budget won't work. And if you aren't *both* represented in the goals, the budget won't work. Intelligent, competent adults won't support a budgeting plan that doesn't have anything they want in it. Not long term, anyway. If your individual goals are not represented, you won't be able to fake it and make the budget work for long—because you are not emotionally invested in it. You may be intellectually invested, but if your dreams, which are now goals, aren't in this budget, you will find every excuse in the world to "bust your budget."

So, get to work. Write, stretch, use your eraser and keep filling in the chart. If it would help you to have more time categories, do that. Will and Diane now have a time category for Australia. Do what helps you to put the puzzle pieces of your life together in a way that works for you both.

When you are done, confirm when you will meet for your next money meeting. The agenda for your next meeting follows this chapter.

And, have fun again this week as you practice budgeting with cash.

Money Meeting #3

W ell, here you are at your third official money meeting. Congratulations! You said you were committed to learning a new way of working with money and now you are showing each other that you really meant what you said. This is what commitment is really about. Commitment means consistently doing what you said you were going to do—day after day, week after week. This consistent behavior creates the third cornerstone of your new money structure—*trust.*

And I just know that you have been learning more about compromise than you ever thought you could—or probably ever wanted to! But you are doing it.

Money Meeting Agenda

1. Set/confirm the time for the next meeting.

2. Evaluate the cash budget you worked with this week. Ask your partner, "So, Dear, what worked this week for you and what didn't work?"

   Then your partner asks you, "So, Honey, what worked for you this week and what didn't work?"

   I'm using this "endearing" language to remind you to keep the conversation respectful and loving—without judgment. You have a commitment to making your money life work, so you must learn to talk to each other lovingly even when you don't do everything perfectly.

Be patient! You will make mistakes. You will miscalculate some categories and just plain screw up sometimes. Give yourselves a break. You're learning.

As you evaluate your cash budget, look at the two parts of budgeting—the management part and the money part—separately.

First, the management part:

• Did you stumble over one of your beliefs and then rationalize a spending decision?

"I did that," says Neil. "I bought a new bike rack with a charge card. I told myself that the rack was on sale. It's easier to mount than my old one. And besides, I make a lot of money and should be able to buy a simple bike rack."

As he hears Anne sigh he continues, "Actually, I still believe all those reasons." He looks at his wife as she shakes her head in frustration. "Wait, Anne, I'm not done, yet. I really do believe all those reasons. And, if I wasn't married to you, it would be all right. Except, of course, I would probably need a second house for all my stuff and then wouldn't have the option of retiring early—which I do now. Even though I hate to admit that, it's true." Neil grins when he sees the amazed look on Anne's face.

"And Neil, I would never know what fun is if I wasn't married to you. I would never have been hiking in Glacier National Park or rock climbing or rafting."

"I know that," Neil says. "I'm really very good for you—I make a lot of money and I'm fun." Anne throws one of the office pillows at Neil, in jest. "See, Ruth, she never lets me finish what I'm saying."

"Anne," Neil continues, "I know that using the credit card broke trust with you. We both agreed to do this and I changed the rules. I know. I really know that there isn't a bike rack in the world that's worth breaking trust with you. I apologize."

Neil grins and says, "I will leave my credit card in the file cabinet in the home office. Ouch! That hurts. But, seriously, I would like to negotiate a raise in my personal money—because, for one thing, bikes are going on sale in the spring."

"I'm willing to talk about that, Neil," Anne responds. "I feel safer even if you get more personal money, because we have rules and I don't have to worry."

So, again, in the management part of your money, ask yourselves if you need to make any changes to make the cash budget work even better. Yes, you will use cash again next week to continue practicing commitment, respect, trust and, of course, compromise.

Second, let's look at the money part of budgeting. Evaluate what worked and what didn't in the money part:

- Did you avoid using the checkbook or a charge card?

- Did you spend *only* cash for all flexible expenses?

- Did you avoid using your couple cash for personal expenses or personal cash for couple expenses?

- Did you avoid pilfering cash from one envelope to pay for an expense that should have been paid from another envelope?

- Was there enough money for the week? Did either of you have to wait to buy something or buy something cheaper because the cash was not there?

- Do you need to adjust the amount of cash in any of the envelopes? If you do, agree on what the changes are so you can practice the cash budget for another week.

3. Review your chapter 9 notes about setting goals. Do you see the need to adjust your goals? Take your time as you think this through. Did either one of you acquiesce—rather than compromise—about a goal? Your goals will be in your "real budget," which you will begin to form in chapter 10. It is essential that you each know and feel that your goals are included in your planning.

4. Go ahead to chapter 10.

Ten

Drawing a Portrait of
Your Money Life

It's time to start putting together the components of a "real budget." You may be saying, "Finally! We get to what this book is supposed to be about." Or, you may have just felt your stomach clutch and your back tighten. You believe life as you have known it is about to end. But I want to assure you, *budget* is not a four-letter word.

Are you ready? Let's get started.

First, get out your goal-setting chart from the end of chapter 9. As you draw a portrait of your money life, you will want to check these sheets from time to time to make sure your goals are included in this portrait. Also, remember that some of your goals may be represented in this budget only symbolically at this point. That is, the amount of money allocated to a specific goal may not be much—for now. That's okay.

Just get your goals into the budget so you know that at some point they will really happen. You and your partner will make them happen.

Next, each of you should open your notebooks to a clean sheet of paper, and again, you will want to have a pencil with a large eraser.

You may want your checkbook register handy to help you remember how you have spent your money. In addition, last year's checkbook registers or your returned checks may be of help. If you have an expense/income information record on your computer, run off a copy. That information could make this process easier. A calculator will help, too.

Each of you should write down all the information you cover in your individual notebooks. This way, you will both be equally clear about the numbers, and in case one of you makes an error, the other will be able to catch it.

Reminder: You are drawing a full portrait of your money life. For this exercise, don't worry which one of you said you would pay which bill, or how much money you said you were going to spend on something. You are not *changing* your system yet. This is simply an exercise in writing down budget numbers to get a comprehensive picture of your money life, including personal expenses and couple/family expenses.

While you are working together, don't forget the four cornerstones you have been practicing: commitment, trust, respect and, of course, compromise.

You will know some of your budget numbers for sure and some will be a calculated guess. The numbers at this stage don't have to be perfectly accurate, but do your best to make them as accurate as possible.

So, let's get started. Step by step, write down the following money information. Be patient. And remember to *be nice* to each other!

Step 1: List Monthly "Fixed" Expenses

Make a list of all your *monthly* bills. These are your basic expenses, known as your *fixed expenses*. They usually cost the same or almost the same each month. You need three pieces of information about each of these expenses:

1. What is the expense?
2. What is the amount of the expense that you have to pay *or* usually pay each month?
3. What is the day of each month that this payment is due?

Name of the Expense	Amount	Due Date
1. Rent/Mortgage	$	
2. Phone service	$	
3. Long distance phone	$	
4. Monthly utilities: <u>electric</u>	$	
5. Monthly utilities: _____	$	
6. Loan payment: <u>car</u>	$	
7. Loan payment: _____	$	
8. Credit card payment: _____	$	

Name of the Expense	Amount	Due Date
9. Credit card payment: _____	$	
10. Parking contract	$	
11.	$	
12.	$	
13. Therapy: group or individual	$	
14. Orthodontic payment	$	
15.	$	
Total Amount of Payments:	$	

Step 2: List Nonmonthly "Have-To" Expenses

Make a list of all the expenses you *have to pay* each *year*. These are not routine monthly expenses but rather those expenses you pay quarterly, twice yearly or yearly. An example is a car insurance premium that must be paid twice a year.

Also list the expenses you *know* you will have to pay sometime, you just don't know *when* or exactly *how much* the expense will be. An example of this kind of expense is car repair. Other examples are the expense of an unexpected visit by a plumber to fix a water leak or the expense of a trip to the dentist because you have a toothache.

These kinds of expenses protect your assets. Your home is

an asset, your car is an asset and your body is an asset. This account will cover medical and dental expenses that are not covered by health insurance or a pretax medical fund at work.

These are expenses that you *have to* pay or something bad will happen. If you don't go to the dentist, your mouth will hurt. If you don't take care of your car, it may break down. If you don't call the plumber, you may have even more problems in your home. It takes money to take care of these assets so you don't lose them.

The best way to estimate these expenses is to look back in last year's checkbook and see how much you spent. You can also talk to someone who may be able to help you estimate these expenses. For example, your auto mechanic may be able to predict what kinds of repair and maintenance your car will need in the coming year.

This step may be more difficult to work through than step 1. Remember, though, that your estimates *don't* have to be perfect. Just make your best guess and it will work out fine.

These nonmonthly expenses are easy to forget about or pretend they won't happen. But it is important to include these expenses if you want your budget to be workable and successful. Not only do many couples forget about these expenses, but many times they are quite large. You don't really have a choice about paying these kinds of expenses. If you don't pay your car insurance, you can't drive your car. So include them.

To complete this step, you need the same three pieces of information you needed in step 1—expense, amount and due date—except that here the amount of the expense should be for the *entire year*. This means if car insurance costs you $350 every six months, you will write $700 in the column marked "Yearly Amount."

Name of the Expense	Yearly Amount	Due Date
1. Car insurance	$700	6/1 & 1/1
2. License plates	$	
3. Car oil changes	$	
4. Car repair	$	
5. Rental insurance	$	
6. Tax preparation	$	
7. Noninsurance: medical	$	
8. Noninsurance: dental	$	
9. Home/apartment repair	$	
10. Life insurance	$	
11. Nonroutine therapy	$	
12.	$	
13.	$	
14.	$	
15. Emergencies	$	
Total Yearly Expenses:	$	

Now, convert the "Total Yearly Expenses" number to a monthly cost, for two reasons:

1. You need to know how much money you need monthly to take care of all your nonmonthly have-to expenses. Otherwise, you will either forget about these expenses or you will live with continual anxiety, knowing the bill is coming but not knowing how to pay it.

2. If you know the monthly amount you will need to cover these nonmonthly have-to expenses, you can "save" money each month so the money is there when you need it.

You turn this yearly cost into a monthly expense simply by dividing it by twelve, because there are twelve months in the year. So, if the "Total Yearly Expenses" number is $1,800, divide this figure by 12 ($1,800 ÷ 12 = $150). So the monthly expense to pay for all the yearly costs is $150.

Calculate this figure for your own situation:

Total Yearly Expenses ÷ 12 = Monthly Expenses for Nonmonthly Have-To Expenses

$_____ ÷ 12 = $_____

Step 3: Add Monthly and Nonmonthly Expenses

Adding your monthly fixed expenses (from step 1) and your nonmonthly have-to expenses (from step 2) gives you your total monthly cost:

$_____	+	$_____	=	$_____
Monthly Fixed Expenses		Monthly Have-to Expenses		Total Monthly Cost of Steps 1 and 2

How are you doing? Does your calculator need new batteries yet?

Do you need to get a cup of tea? Or maybe an aspirin?

Are you being patient? Are you being nice to each other? You may want to take a five-minute break. You have done good work.

Ready to continue? Let's do it.

Step 4: List Weekly "Flexible" Expenses

Write down the amount of money you are using in your cash budget each week, including how much you have individually to spend and how much is for couple/family expenses.

Weekly Cash	Yours	Mine	Ours
Weekly Totals			

Now add the three columns to get the total weekly amount you need for your cash budget:

$_____$ + $_____$ + $_____$ = $_____$

   Yours   +   Mine   +   Ours   =   Cash Needed Weekly

Again, you need to convert this weekly amount into a *monthly* amount for your budget. To do this, multiply the weekly amount by 4.3. You cannot simply multiply by four weeks because over the course of a year, there are 4.3 weeks in a month. So, if your weekly cash amount is $100, your monthly budgeting number is $430 ($100 X 4.3 = $430).

Now you do it:

Weekly Amount X 4.3 = $_____

Step 5: List Nonmonthly "Choice" Expenses

List all the other expenses missing in this budget. These include both monthly and yearly expenses that are important, but you have more choice about *what*, *when* and *how much* money you spend on these items. In budgeting language, these expenses are called your *annual flexible expenses*. You need two pieces of information about these items:

1. The name of the expense.
2. An estimate of how much you spend each year on the item.

Expense	Amount	Yearly Estimate
1. Donations	$	$
2. Major entertaining	$	$
3. Major holidays	$	$
4. Vacations/travel	$	$
5. Home furnishings	$	$
6. Birthdays	$	$
7.	$	$
8.	$	$
Total Annual Flexible Expenses	$	$

Now, divide this annual cost by 12 to get a monthly amount for your monthly budget—just as you did in step 2:

Total Monthly Flexible Expenses = $_____

Step 6: Calculate a Grand Total

Add your figures from steps 3, 4 and 5 to get a grand total of monthly expenses:

Monthly Expenses (total of fixed monthly and non-monthly have-tos; see step 3): $_____

+

Weekly Flexible Expenses (your weekly expenses x 4.3 weeks; see step 4):

$_____

+

Nonmonthly Choice Expenses (step 5): $_____

=

Monthly Expenses Grand Total: $_____

Wait a minute. Double-check your goal sheets. Are your goals really in this budget? If they are, continue. If they are not, take a few minutes to get them in the budget.

Congratulations! You have completed the expense part of your financial portrait.

And, more important, you are done for the day. Yes, this is true. You need to stop now. You are probably both exhausted, and if you keep going you will have trouble being patient with each other—you will have trouble being nice.

Don't forget, budgeting is an evolutionary process. It will take time to form a new money plan. Meanwhile, you are practicing the cornerstones of your new money structure—commitment, respect, trust and compromise—and you are practicing actual budgeting skills with your cash. If you continue working on the budget now, you may erode some of the progress you have made. Trust me. It's time to stop.

Before you leave, though, confirm the date and time of your next money meeting. If you need additional information to complete the charts in this chapter, decide who will get what information before the next meeting. Continue to use cash as a budgeting tool until the next meeting.

The agenda for your next money meeting is next.

Money Meeting #4

⌒

Well here you are, keeping your commitment for the fourth time. I hope you are as impressed with yourselves as I am. You said you were committed to learning a new way of working with money, and again you are showing each other that you really meant what you said. Congratulations!

Money Meeting Agenda

1. Set/confirm the time for your next money meeting.

2. Evaluate your weekly cash budget. What is working and what isn't? What do you need to change in the cash budget so you can continue to practice commitment, respect, trust and compromise?

3. If you needed additional information to complete chapter 10, did you get it? If you did, go back and add the numbers or information so each category is complete. If you did not get the information you need, decide who will get it by the next meeting.

4. Continue this meeting by working through chapter 11 together.

Eleven

If You Get Yours, Will I Get Mine?

You need to follow two absolute rules in order to make a budget work. The first rule of budgeting is: *The numbers in the budget have to work.* We will work with the second rule of budgeting in chapter 12.

In this chapter, you will learn how to follow the first rule as you practice the cornerstone of creative compromise—this chapter will really give you a chance to practice stretching!

Making the numbers in your budget work means that the numbers have to balance with the amount of money you have to spend. Simple? Oh, yes. Difficult? Enormously. Imperative for your money life to work? Absolutely! You cannot avoid this step if you want your money life to work.

In addition, you have to balance your budget with the goals you identified in chapter 9. Remember, these goals must be part of the budget or you won't have the motivation to make it work in the long term. Speaking of compromise, you may need to adjust your goals to make the numbers work—for example, putting them into a longer time frame. But don't forget to include them.

Crunching the Numbers

You need to sit down together and crunch the numbers in your budget, item by item, until the total amount of money you need in your life does not exceed your spendable income.

Just so you are in agreement about what *spendable income* really is, let's define it:

Your total (gross) income	$_____
–	
The amount you are putting away for retirement	$_____
–	
The cost of your tax-deductible benefits (such as pretax accounts for health care and child care)	$_____
–	
The cost of your total income taxes	$_____
–	
Any other automatic deductions you have (such as union dues, life insurance)	$_____
=	
Your spendable (net) income	$_____

This final number, spendable income, is the number you will use for budgeting—whether you are a salaried person or self-employed. If you are retired, simply use the amount of your after-tax income.

For now, you need to simply agree on the amount of income that is available to spend. Sometimes couples don't find it so easy to agree on this amount:

"This isn't as easy as you think, Ruth," says Neil. "Anne would put all of our money into retirement, except for some measly amount to live on. We simply can't agree on that number. I have maxed out the 401(k) plan at work and that still isn't enough for her."

"You're exaggerating, again," says Anne. "But he's right on one thing, Ruth. We can't agree on what spendable income really is. And, I'm tired of fighting with him and I'm scared about our future if I don't hold the line here."

If you cannot agree on how much to put away for retirement or how much you need to spend on benefits, call in the professionals to reach a compromise. Each of you should make at least one appointment with a professional—of your own choosing—who works with retirement planning and benefits. *Both* of you should go to *both* appointments—so you can *both* hear the information. If you still cannot agree, set two more appointments—one each. Eventually, you will find a legitimate compromise so you can make a decision about how much to put away for the future. Then, you will be able to move forward with your budgeting.

There is no shortcut here. You are making an investment in your future as a couple, and you must take the time to do this work. Some couples think I just don't realize how busy they are. I do understand what it means to have a full life, but you need to take the time to make your money life work as a couple. You will make the time for this work if you decide it is a priority. If you need to remind yourself *why* it should be a priority and why you are working through this book, go back in your notebooks and read what you have written over the past weeks.

Now, keep going by writing down the amount of money you have available monthly as spendable income. Add to this number any other sources of income, such as earned income, child support income, maintenance income and investment income. Don't include *possible* income, such as a gift or a bonus or profit sharing. These are all variable. Use the following chart to track all sources of spendable income:

Source of Money	Monthly Amount
1. Paycheck—yours (spendable amount)	$
2. Paycheck—mine (spendable amount)	$
3. Fixed income from investments	$
4. Child support money received	$
5.	$
6.	$
7.	$
Total Monthly Spendable (Net) Income:	$

Now, go back to chapter 10 to find the grand total of your monthly expenses that you calculated. Write that down:

Grand Total of Monthly Expenses $_____

Now, subtract your total monthly expenses from your total monthly spendable income:

$_____	–	$_____	=	$_____
Total Monthly Income		**Total Monthly Expenses**		

This final number is the difference between the money you have available to spend and the amount of your expenses. This final number will result in one of three scenarios: (1) the number is zero, (2) the number is positive or (3) the number is negative. Let's look at each of these scenarios.

Scenario #1: The Number Is Zero

This is the easiest scenario to deal with. If the number is zero you are spending exactly what you have available to spend.

If you are pleased with your lifestyle and don't want to make any changes in this lifestyle, and *if* your goals are integrated into your budget and will happen in the time frame you are planning (including retirement), then you don't *need* to make any changes. Your expenses match your income, so you are done with this chapter. Congratulations!

Before you wrap up this meeting, make sure you know when you will meet again (the agenda for this next meeting follows this chapter). And, keep using the weekly cash budget.

Scenario #2: The Number Is Positive

This scenario is the most fun. If the number is positive, you have more money available to spend than what you need for the expenses you have identified. You have moved beyond the first step in money planning. This first step is the stabilization step: what matters is that everything is being paid, and no further debt is being accumulated to maintain your lifestyle. The second step, which you are now in, is called growth. In this growth step, you may want to increase your expenses in three possible areas. As you decide what to do, don't forget the language of compromise if the decision making gets difficult.

First Possibility: If you have credit card debt, bank loans, car loans or any other debt, including a mortgage, you may want to increase your payments. For example, you may decide to double or triple the payment you are making to your credit card. To do this, go back to chapter 10 to the first sheet of your practice budget and increase the payments to those debts you have decided to pay off. Write these new payments into your list of fixed expenses. Now readjust the grand total.

Second Possibility: You may want to increase your retirement savings. It may be helpful to talk to a professional about additional ways to accumulate money for your retirement. Increasing the amount of money you save for retirement gives you more choices when you are older. If this is your decision, go back and adjust the spendable income figure and subtract again to get a new bottom number.

Third Possibility: You may want to start a savings account just to save. This account doesn't have a spending agenda. Now, that's a new concept! Money that you deposit into this account just sits there so you can feel financially secure. It is *not* for paying your car insurance or for a vacation or a new coat. It just sits in this account.

In budgeting language, this is your emergency savings account. Your budget already covers repairs, insurances and all the other nonmonthly expenses. The money in this emergency savings account will only be used if you need income replacement, that is, if one of you is unable to earn your income. If you have disability insurance, this account will cover the elimination period in the policy—the period after you are disabled and before the insurance starts to pay.

Let's hope that you never need this money, but each month you will add to this account and watch these savings grow and create nonretirement security for you.

This account is rather like the safety net under a tightrope walker at a circus. The tightrope walker has trained and plans to walk safely across the tightrope, just as you have been practicing and planning your budget so it will work.

The tightrope walker also has a balancing pole in her hands and people spotting her on either side of the rope, which increase her chances of successfully walking across the tightrope. You also have taken special precautions that your budget will work by calculating all the expenses you normally have during the year.

But if the worst comes to pass and the tightrope walker—with all her skills, training and planning—slips and falls, it is not a disaster. She falls into a safety net in place just for this occasion. You also, with all your developing management skills and money calculations, may also slip. You may not be able to work for income. Or some crisis may happen that there was no way to prepare for. You also have a safety net. A disaster won't occur. A safety net is a reassuring and necessary part of budgeting.

If you decide to start an emergency savings account, add the amount you plan to save to your fixed monthly expense list in chapter 10. Then, recalculate your budget.

When you have made all the adjustments, you are done with your money meeting for the week. Before you leave, though, remind each other of the date and time of your next weekly meeting (the agenda for this meeting follows this chapter). Continue to use cash for your weekly budget.

Scenario #3: The Number Is Negative

This scenario is the most difficult. If the number is negative, your expenses are greater than the amount of money you have available to spend each month. This scenario really gives you an opportunity to practice the skill of compromise as you work to stabilize your money life.

- A negative number means that you probably struggle to pay your bills each month.

- A negative number means that the car insurance bill probably surprises you when it comes in the mail.

- A negative number means you often get discouraged as you try to figure out how to pay a bill.

- A negative number means you probably use credit to make up the difference between your income and expenses. Because of this, you may have more debt than you ever thought you would—credit cards, home equity loans, lines of credit.

- A negative number means you probably are spending a great deal of your time blaming each other and resenting each other.

It's time to make the numbers work as you practice the skill of compromise. You can do this! You have to do this if you are going to change how you work with money in your life.

Balancing a budget is a very simple job. Either you *increase* your income—the money you have to spend—or *decrease* your expenses—the money you are spending—or you do a little of each.

Making the numbers work when the bottom line of your budget is a negative number is a simple but very difficult job. But you have done difficult jobs before. You can do this difficult job, too!

First, is there any way you can increase your income? Can you do this without hurting your health—or your relationship? Is there anything you can do to bring in some additional money that will either get rid of the negative number or at least reduce it a bit? What would it be? How much money would it add to your monthly income? How soon can you start? What specifically can each of you do to contribute to increased income?

Next, go through your lists of expenses, item by item, in chapter 10. Is there any way you can reduce expenses? Can you reduce any of your utilities? How? Remember, be nice to each other!

Take your time. Find ways, large and small, to reduce expenses. Remember to practice compromising—how can you each get what is important to you and to your relationship and still make the numbers in the budget work.

When you're finished, recalculate the budget figures, both the new income figures and the new expense figures. If your new final number is zero, you are done.

If you're like most couples, though, you still have a negative number because you did not make enough changes. So, keep working. You have to make the numbers work or you are setting yourselves up for failure. You've worked too hard to give up now. You can change your money life, if you are willing to make difficult decisions at this stage of the process.

Don't get stuck at this point like Will and Diane feel they are:

"Well, Ruth," says Diane, "we still have a negative number and we're stuck."

"I think we've made the easy decisions and now we're afraid to go any further," interrupts Will, "because we'll end up in a fight. And I'm tired of fighting."

What Diane and Will don't see is that they will continue to fight if they don't keep going. If the numbers don't balance, eventually—tomorrow or next month—they will have trouble paying their bills and then will find themselves back in the same old place—fighting. They need to do it differently this time so the results can be different.

Doing it differently means that you have to be willing to compromise. If you are going to get what you need both individually and as a couple, you must be willing to really stretch into new territory—into new ways to earn money and new ways to decrease expenses.

Remember that compromise doesn't mean losing. In fact, if you *don't* compromise, you *will* lose. Compromise means doing things differently so that you don't lose your relationship, your financial security or your happiness. Compromise means you are willing to try new ways to make this work.

So, take a deep breath and go through the numbers again. Is there anything you can do to earn more money, even on a temporary basis? Brainstorm! Get creative! Can you rent a room in your house to a college student? Or rent part of your garage? Do you need to ask for a raise at work or raise your fees if you are self-employed? Do you need to work more hours so you can make more money? Does anyone owe you money that you could collect? How about a garage sale? What about that set of china that you'll never use—could you sell it? How about a part-time sales job? There has to be a way to increase the money you have available.

Now, go through your expenses and do the same kind of brainstorming. Is there any way to lower the cost of your groceries? Can you shop at a less expensive grocery store? Can you write menus to reduce food waste?

Can you eat out less? Can you change the cost of day care? Can you get by—just for a while—with one car? Can you put up with the inconvenience of riding the bus or carpooling to make this work?

Can you reduce any of your health care expenses without hurting yourselves? Do you really need those magazines and newspapers? Do you really need to spend that amount on laundry and dry cleaning? Or on clothes? Or on entertainment?

Come on! Where can you make changes? Can you mow your own lawn instead of hiring someone to do it? Can you both be responsible for cleaning the house so you don't need to hire someone to do it? Maybe you can't afford to live where you do. Can you increase the deductible on your car insurance to reduce your premiums?

Please don't give up! Keep working with the figures until the bottom line is zero. You owe it to yourself, to each other and to your future to succeed.

If you absolutely cannot get that number to zero, take a break for a few hours or even a few days. You will feel more creative after you have had a break. So, put the numbers away. Commit to a time *before* the next weekly money meeting so you can work with these numbers again.

You are done for today. Your budget is evolving—congratulations!

Before you go, confirm the date, time and place of your next money meeting. (The agenda for that meeting follows this chapter.) Continue using cash until the next meeting.

Money Meeting #5

You have now met for five scheduled money meetings. If you have been able to meet for five weeks in a row, you really have changed a pattern. You really have made the decision to make your money life work with a new model—a model of partnership.

If your budget is not quite balanced yet and you're feeling stuck, let it go for now. Work through chapter 12. It may give you the impetus to really make your budget numbers work.

Money Meeting Agenda

1. Set/confirm the day and time of your next weekly money meeting.

2. Make any adjustments needed in your cash budget. The practice you are getting with this cash budget is invaluable, so keep it up.

3. Go ahead to chapter 12.

Twelve

What's This All About, Anyway?

Y ou're lucky we're back, Ruth," David says. "After that last assignment, I thought Julie or I, or both of us, would bail out. It's the most discouraging assignment we've ever had."

David and Julie need to know, just as you may need to know, that it takes an enormous amount of courage to complete that last assignment. Many couples get so discouraged when they see the bottom line in their budget that they give up. They never complete the assignment, and they never change their money life. They just continue to be discouraged. Completing that assignment is like facing down the bogeymonster. How bad are the numbers, really?

Completing the budgeting assignment means facing up to the issue so you can deal with it. If you never face it, you will never solve it. You will never change your money life. The years will go by and you will continue to hold out hope that either the circumstances will change or your partner will change. This doesn't work—it hasn't worked yet and won't in the future.

If you never face it, you will never solve it.

"We sure found that out," says Diane. "We thought when the car was paid off we could get ahead. Didn't happen. Then we thought that when our older child got out of day care, that would free up a lot of money. Didn't happen, again. Then I thought if Will could just get a raise, but that didn't work either."

"We even refinanced the house," Will adds. "Our payment went down by almost $200 per month and even that didn't seem to make any difference. Nothing seemed to help for long."

Fixing Your Money Life from the Inside

If you are waiting for something to change your money life—some event like a change in day care, refinancing the house, a raise, some epiphany that your partner will have so the spending stops—it won't happen. No outside circumstances will change your money life over the long term.

Your money life needs to be fixed from the inside—by *both* of you. Then you can fix the outside. You have been making inside changes as you work through this book. You identified in chapter 11 how big of a money problem you really have. And, you decided what you were going to do about it, starting now. You have decided not to wait for something outside of you to fix it. You are fixing your money problems together—today—from the inside out.

> **Your money life needs to be fixed from the inside—by *both* of you. Then you can fix the outside.**

"You're right," says Julie. "We have a negative number in our budget. And no matter what we cut, we still don't have enough money. At least we understand now why we need the credit cards every month."

Using credit cards to bridge the gap between your income and expenses doesn't work over the long term. Eventually the debt gets out of hand. You need more and more money just to pay the minimum payments on each card, without really getting ahead. Soon you may not have enough money to pay the debt payments *and* your other expenses. So you charge more and more each month to maintain the same standard of living.

It feels like a trap. If you don't want to be trapped and if you want to be able to reach your goals and have a healthy financial life together, then you need to make your budget work without credit cards.

"That's easy for you to say, Ruth," David comments. "It looks like I'm going to have to give up my Saturday golf game and probably even my underground parking if we're going to do what I think we have to do."

"See, here he goes," sighs Julie. "His precious golf and his precious heated parking spot. He'll never give those up."

"What about you?" asks David, his voice rising. "What

about those classes you take or the added afternoon of day care or the books or the clothes?"

David and Julie are both assuming that they will have to give up what is important to them. They both believe that to make their budget balance, they will have to give up what gives them pleasure and freedom. David believes that if Julie gets what she wants, he won't get what he wants. And Julie believes that if David gets what he wants, she won't get what is important to her.

They are both wrong! What *is* true is that if David and Julie don't get their budget to balance, they will lose what they really want and need. Remember the commitment you made? *Without blame, you have decided to learn a new way of working together in your money life.*

While Julie and David are fussing and feuding over golf games and classes and parking spaces and child care, they are forgetting that these are not the most important things in life. Maybe you forgot that, too.

All couples can work out these details—the parking, the golf, the child care. As important as these issues are, they are still details. What is *really* important is that couples remember their commitment to learn to work together.

The Second Rule of Budgeting

In chapter 11, you learned the first rule of budgeting: The numbers in the budget have to work. This means the numbers have to balance—your spending cannot exceed your income.

This brings us to the second rule of budgeting: *The budgeting choices you make must feel fair to both of you.* With the four corner-stones of your new money structure in place—commitment, trust, respect and compromise—you have to make your budget work not just in numbers but also in feelings.

That's where David and Julie are stuck, maybe just like you. They can add and subtract and cut and paste their budget until the bottom numbers balance. But what they are arguing about has nothing to do with their mathematical skills. They are arguing about *what* they will cut and *who* will pay the price. This cutting job cannot be done unless it feels fair to both of you.

"Impossible!" David explodes. "Absolutely impossible. The price we pay to balance this budget will never feel fair—to either one of us. Never."

But it has to. If the budget doesn't feel fair to both of you, all of the work you have done so far will fall apart. Nothing you have built throughout this book—including commitment, respect, trust and compromise—can hold up in the face of the feeling of unfairness. The feeling of unfairness builds resentment as day after day you say to yourself, and sometimes to your partner, "This isn't fair. It really isn't."

Nothing destroys relationships more than the quiet killer called resentment. So unless the budget you are forming feels fair to both of you, it just won't work.

> **Nothing destroys relationships more than the quiet killer called resentment.**

"Well, then," Julie says quietly, "tell us how to do this, because we certainly have a lot of resentment in our relationship. And, at least for me, that anger has gotten even worse since we balanced the budget. I feel like the kids and I were cut out."

"*You* were cut out!" David interrupts. "*I'm* the one who got cut out. There's no money for my fall fishing trip with my buddies. And I'll probably be able to swing my clubs only once a month."

David and Julie are stuck, maybe like you. They are stuck in resentment, and this makes it impossible to make their budget work. The only way to make a budget work without resentment is to compromise so the numbers feel fair to both of you. The only way to make this happen is to get a broader perspective on your life.

Sometimes it seems that couples working to balance their budgets are looking at a very large elephant. But one person is looking at one of the elephant's front feet, and the other is looking at one of the elephant's back feet. Each thinks that this perspective is giving them a clear picture of what an elephant looks like. Both think they are right, but they're both wrong.

The trick is to get this couple to look upward and see what this large elephant really looks like. The elephant's feet, while certainly an important part of the animal, are only a small part of the elephant. Likewise, any couple's life together is much bigger than their own individual perspectives. Couples need to teach themselves to broaden their perspectives.

To make the second rule of budgeting work, to make the budgeting choices you make feel fair to both of you, you need to get a bigger picture of your life—a broader perspective.

Let's try to broaden this perspective, working individually.

Exercise: Broadening Your Perspective

Working individually, write "Chapter 12" at the top of a clean page in your notebook and work through the following questions:

1. What age will you be when you consider yourself to be old? This should be an age where your life will be quite different from today. The "elephant's foot" you will be fussing about at the age you call "old" will be quite different from the "elephant's foot" you are fussing about today.

2. Now, think quietly for a moment as you—from this "old" age perspective—look back on your life. Write your responses to the following questions in your notebook:

   • Think back to when you were in high school, or maybe college, and to when you got your first real job, got married and maybe had children. Who were your friends? What did you do in your free time? How did you spend the greatest share of your money?

   • Whom did you help and why? Whom didn't you help and why?

   • How did you spend most of your time? Whom did you love?

   • What hurt you? What do you still grieve—today? What do you wish you had done that you didn't?

3. Continue writing in your notebook, answering the questions from the perspective of old age:

- What kinds of experiences gave you the most joy? The most satisfaction? What kinds of experiences do you wish you had spent more time doing? Why?

- What experiences give you regrets? If you could change what you did, what would you change? Why?

- How did you make spending choices with your money? Do you wish you had spent your money differently? How would you have spent it? Why?

4. Still in a thoughtful frame of mind, picture your death at an even older age and answer these questions in your notebook, still working individually:

- What do you want to be remembered for and why? Be specific.

- What do you want to make sure you do not forget to do? To have? To be? Why?

5. Now, still working individually, take a deep breath as you review your answers to all of the questions. List your responses to the questions in order based on their importance to you.

Number 1: Most important—have to make sure.

Number 2: Next important— can't forget about.

Number 3:

Number 4:

And so on.

You have just made a list of your *personal values*. Values can be about partnership, love and family. They can be about security, including financial security. They can be about God, spirituality or a higher power. Values can be about fun and happiness. They can be about education. Your list reflects your values, based on what you have learned about your life from the perspective of old age.

Here's what some of the couples you've met in this book have identified as important values:

"My number-one value," Jack says, "is to make sure Maria and I are still married and my two sons spend time with us. I guess I forget that as I'm working to make my dream—my business—work, I need to make sure I don't lose the three people who are most important to me."

"I listed security for our family as my number-one value," says Julie, sounding very serious. "I just want our children to not worry about whether David and I will stay married, and I don't want them to have to worry about whether we can pay our bills."

"I want to make sure Neil and I have fun together while we are still relatively young," says Anne. "My number-one value is fun and my number-two value is money for retirement."

Neil interrupts with a grin, "Well, Anne, my number-one value is money for retirement. I want to make sure we really have enough. And my number-two value is for us to travel and play now."

When Neil and Anne listed their values, they surprised themselves by reversing the roles they played when talking about budgeting. When they were able to get a broader perspective on their lives, each of their priorities changed.

Each of these couples, maybe just like you, has started looking at life and at money with a new and broader perspective.

Now, look at your list of values. Think about how you spent your time this week. Did these values play a large part in your time commitments? Think about how you spent your money this week and then this month? Did your spending reflect your values?

Think about how you interacted with your children this week or your friends. Were your values there? Were your values in place during your interactions with your partner—the one sitting right there next to you!

In your notebooks, write a statement to yourself that begins this way:

"The areas where my values show in my daily life are
_____."

Write a second statement to yourself that begins this way:

"The areas where my values are not represented in my daily life are _____."

Write a third statement to yourself that begins this way:

"The changes I need to make in my life in order to live my values on a daily basis are _____
_____."

You need to make these changes now so that when you reach the age you now call "old" you will know that you have lived your life with purpose—based on your values.

Now it's time to see if you can come up with a list of values that you are both intellectually and emotionally willing to support. These are your *partnership values*.

Exercise: Identifying Your Partnership Values

Take the time now to read your individual value lists to each other. Then share your three statements about values.

If you are like most couples, your values are not that different from each other. They may fall in a different order, but you are probably more similar than different in your values.

1. Look at both of your lists. Can you agree on the most important value to you as a couple? Without this value, nothing else really matters. Without this value, life will be full of regrets when you are at the age you called "old."

2. What is your second-most important value as a couple? Continue working together to list your partnership values. Remember the skill of compromise—stretching—when deciding what priority each value has. Remember the skill of compromise when deciding how to put these values into words that work for both of you.

Your list of partnership values reflects what *really* matters when you look at your life from a broader perspective. The other things in your life are simply details—important, of course, but details. Are these details the reason for living and being together? Of course not! It's your list of values that is the foundation for all your budget planning together.

Remember that your budget is simply a tool to make your goals happen. Goals are measurable. You know when you have reached a goal and when you have not. Values, however, by themselves, are not measurable. That's why so many older people have such serious regrets about their lives. They have regrets because they cannot find their values in how they lived their lives. This incongruity between what they thought they would do with their lives and what they actually did creates great sadness for many people.

Your values need to be included in your budget planning so you can be sure they're not just words but the foundation of your life. For your life to really reflect your values, you need a budget that integrates your goals, which are anchored by your foundation of commitment, respect, trust and compromise.

Exercise: Writing a Value Statement for Your Partnership

Together, write a partnership value statement. You can also call this a partnership mission statement. The purpose of this statement is to say:

"This is why we are living our life this way—together. This is how we want to be remembered. This is our legacy."

Be careful here. Don't make this an intellectual statement. It isn't. This statement needs to come from your heart. It is emotion-based. When you write it and when you read it back, you will be able to feel its impact.

Julie and David's value statement reads, in part: "Our deepest value is to show each other that we cherish each other. We want to know that when we are old, we will still be together and enjoying each other. We want our children to know we cherish them. We want to be financially solvent now and when we're old."

Part of Neil and Anne's statement reads: "We want to have the money to enjoy each other and to travel the world now and when we're old. We want to be remembered for our generous giving to those in need."

Maria and Jack wrote: "We want our life to reflect our deep faith in God. We also want others to see the love we have for each other and our children. We want to create financial security now and in retirement."

Now, ask yourselves: What changes are you going to make as a couple so your daily life, including your money life, is congruent with your value statement?

Here are some of the changes Julie and David plan to make:

- Have a weekly date night. This night is simply to enjoy each other. We can't talk about money or kids or the house. This night is just ours.

- We will not fight in front of the children anymore. That's a rule.

- We will talk to someone at the bank about getting a second mortgage to consolidate our credit card debt. We will close all our credit cards except for one bank card. We will not use this card. We will keep it in the back of the file cabinet. We will stay on budget so we can get our bills paid on time. This is a component of our partnership value to be financially safe.

Neil and Anne's list includes these changes:

- We will stay within our budget so we know we have enough money to enjoy ourselves now and when we retire.
- We will dramatically increase the amount of money we budget for charitable giving.
- When Neil gets his bonus, we will put one-half of the money into our already existing travel savings account. We now call this our "See the World" account. The other half of the bonus will go to charitable giving.
- We will make an appointment with an estate attorney to find out about charitable giving with our estate money.

The following are part of Jack and Maria's list of changes they want to make:

- We will show through our life together our deep love for each other and our faith in God.
- Sundays will be church and family day. We will learn to relax together and to play together. No work on Sunday. No money meetings on Sunday.
- Jack will make an appointment with a business advisor he knows about. He will ask the advisor to help him form a business plan and a business budget. He will also ask the advisor to help him find a way to get funds for his business when he needs them without using the equity in the house or credit cards. Maria will get a copy of the plan and the budget. Jack will keep her informed of his progress in their weekly money meetings.

- We will talk with our banker about refinancing the mortgage to include the debt from the equity loan. If we re-
  finance, we will pay less per month, and the debt will
  eventually be paid in full. We both want to know we are
  financially secure.

Now it's your turn. What will you agree to do to make
your daily life congruent with your partnership values list?
Be specific.

Agreement #1: _____

_____

Agreement #2: _____

_____

Agreement #3: _____

_____

Agreement #4: _____

_____

With these agreements in front of you, look at your budget.
Where are you willing to compromise—to stretch—to make
the details of your budget work? Come on! We aren't talking
about giving up or acquiescing. We are talking about purposeful, value-based decision making. You are doing this to
make your broader perspective of your life work with the daily
details of your life.

- Is that computer, that kind of car, that couch, that dinner
  out, that kind of birthday party for your child really necessary, based on the values you have said you want to live by?

- Is where you park really important in the long run, or is it simply a convenience that really isn't terribly important?
- Can you spend less money so your budget can be balanced *and* you can live congruently with your values?
- Can you earn more money so your budget can be balanced *and* you can live congruently with your values?

Look back at the work you did in chapter 11. With your values list in place, what changes are you willing to make so your daily life is congruent with your partnership values?

In your notebook, list specific changes you will make in your *expenses* and in your *income* in order to make your budget balance in a way that is congruent with your values. You are creatively compromising on life's details so your whole life has meaning.

You are creatively compromising on life's details so your whole life has meaning.

Good work! It's starting to feel fairer, isn't it? Now you feel a bigger purpose—a more important reason—for why you are doing this work. You, like many couples, get so caught up in the dailiness of life that you forget about why you are here and what is really important to you. Your partnership values are what is important. Feels good, doesn't it?

If it doesn't feel good or doesn't feel fairer to you, go through this chapter again. Rework your values until you *know* what you are doing is congruent with your partnership values.

Before you go:

1. Set the time and place for your next money meeting. (The agenda for this meeting follows this chapter.)
2. Continue to practice budgeting with cash.
3. Keep your list of partnership values posted in at least one place this week—in your daily planner, on the refrigerator or on the dashboard of your car. Keep your partnership value statement in mind this week, and watch how it changes your perspective at home and at work as you make money and time decisions.
4. If you did not finish balancing your budget in chapter 11, go back now and make the decisions you need to for the numbers to work *and* feel fair to you both. Be sure to keep your values list in front of you while you work.

Money Meeting #6

Your *sixth* money meeting—you're making this quite a habit, aren't you? I hope that after working through chapter 12, you are feeling more committed—on a deeper level—to each other and your partnership. You may be able to feel this deeper commitment as you realize that you do not feel as resentful. Maybe you are feeling less rigid—less entrenched in getting *your* needs met *your* way. This sense of flexibility is healthy. It means you are truly internalizing the four cornerstones of commitment, respect, trust and the flexibility that comes from compromise.

Money Meeting Agenda

1. Set/confirm the time of your next weekly money meeting.

2. If you have any parts of the budget to finish—either in the numbers or in negotiating fairness—do this before you move on to the next chapter.

3. Continue practicing your weekly cash budget.

4. Continue on now with chapter 13.

Thirteen

Yours, Mine
or Ours?

This chapter is about responsibility. You are probably already feeling extremely responsible for completing twelve chapters in this book so far. And you are responsible—you really are!

The kind of responsibility I'm talking about right now involves making a decision about *who*, specifically, is responsible for *what* in your evolving budget. This sounds simple, but you may find that this step is quite difficult.

It wasn't possible to make this decision until all four cornerstones—commitment, respect, trust and compromise—were in place supporting your new way of working with money. But now it's time.

This chapter is *not* about the logistics of your evolving budget. It's *not* about what bank account the money is in or who will actually write out the checks to pay bills. This chapter *is* about deciding who has responsibility for what. You will answer the question, "Is it *your* responsibility, *my* responsibility or *our* responsibility?" This responsibility covers both your budgeted expenses and your income:

- Is this your expense, my expense or an expense that we share?

- What income are you responsible for—how much and when?

- What income am I responsible for—how much and when?

"That's not a problem for us," says David. "Julie doesn't earn any money. I earn all the money and pay all the essential bills. I give her an amount each month to spend on the rest of the stuff."

"That's the problem," says Julie. "Sometimes you give me what you say you will and sometimes you don't. I don't have any say in how much I get. You just tell me that I should be able to pay for everything; after all, *you* are paying all the *real* bills."

"And sometimes those real bills cost more than I thought," David says heatedly.

"And sometimes," Julie shoots back, "my expenses cost more. Besides," she says softly, "I feel like a child. You're giving me money. It's our money, David. Not just yours to give to me."

This responsibility step isn't so easy, is it? Not even for single-income couples.

Showing the Values of Partnership

Remember the values you identified in chapter 12? And your partnership value statement? A partnership consists of two equal adults. Equal doesn't mean the same. You don't look the same, or act the same or do the same things well. Each of you has a different role to play in your relationship. Each of you is responsible for different things. Sometimes one partner earns income, and sometimes both do. But each values what the other person does. Partners are equal in that they are both adults—this is not a parent-child relationship. Both share equal authority in making the money decisions. That is what a partnership is.

"Ruth, that's not the system we worked out," David explains. "I earn all the income right now, and Julie and I decided that 70 percent of the money decisions would be mine, and she gets the other 30 percent. I think I'm more generous than most men, and at least we're being honest about it. Most couples I know just assume the guy is in charge if he earns the money. They don't talk about it. At least we acknowledge that even though she doesn't earn any money she gets some say, even though it's less than me."

Julie looks at me and says, "I feel like a child. I feel like I have to ask 'Daddy' if I can have money for something. He listens to what I want and why and then decides. Just like that! He decides—yes or no. The discussion is over."

"I'm always one down with David," Julie continues. "I get so frustrated sometimes that I just take the charge card and buy what I need. I know he will blow up later and accuse me of driving us into bankruptcy, but I do it anyway. All day while he's at work earning the money, I'm taking care of the kids and the house. I'm even taking a class right now. I think I work just as hard as he does. I just don't earn any money."

Julie and David need to go back and look at their values. None of their values say, "Taking care of the children has less value than earning the income." None of their values say, "The person who earns the most income has the most power."

Their values, probably like yours, are about partnership, family, financial security, health and spirituality. None of their values say anything about money being the most important. Your values probably don't represent an unequal partnership and state that one of you is above the other.

"That's not a problem for us," Kate explains. "We both earn money. We have individual checkbooks and we have equal responsibility for our bills. We split everything fifty-fifty, and we both have to agree before we take on a new bill. No one has more say than the other. After we pay our share of the bills, we do whatever we want with the money we have left in our own checkbooks."

"It works," Larry adds, "because *you* have enough money left in your checkbook to do something. Your job has always paid more and it probably always will. But I'm absolutely broke. We'd never go out to eat if you didn't pay for it." Larry's voice shakes with restrained emotion as he continues. "We'd never take a trip unless you paid for it. And, even though you've been very generous, you always decide what we're going to do and when. I don't have any real say. You have nice clothes. I don't. You drive a nice car. I don't. You give me great presents, and I can't give you much of anything. It feels awful."

Larry and Kate have an economic class system within their relationship. Even though, on paper, it looks like this system should work and feel fair, it doesn't. This system says that whoever earns the most money has the best lifestyle—the best stuff. Whoever earns the most gets to decide what to do and when.

Although Kate and Larry's system is different from David and Julie's system, neither system creates a partnership. All couples have some kind of income discrepancy between them. The discrepancy can be small—as when one person earns 40 percent of the household income and the other earns 60 percent—or the discrepancy can be large—as when one person earns 100 percent of the income. Also, the roles each member of a couple play in the home are never exactly equal. No two people give absolutely equal contributions—in money, in time and in tasks—to the relationship and to their home. The word *equal* is not a way to measure contributions, including money.

Like Kate and Larry, when "equal" is used to determine a budget, it only feels fair to one of the partners. The other starts to resent the lack of fairness. And, like David and Julie, the parent-child model doesn't work. This model also causes resentment.

Recall from chapter 12 the second rule of budgeting: The budgeting choices you make must *feel* fair to both of you. In that chapter you also learned that resentment is the "quiet killer" of a partnership. You don't want resentment to be the by-product of your budget.

Many times I have trouble figuring out if the couples that come to see me are actually married or in the process of divorce. What creates this confusion for me is that many times the structure of their money lives looks like it was set up by a divorce decree. For example, I hear, "I will give you this much money each month to pay for the expenses of running the house and the children." Doesn't that sound like an alimony or child support agreement? I might also hear, "I will pay for one-half of all the medical bills and education costs for the children." These are interesting money agreements for two people in a long-term committed partnership, aren't they?

Trusting Each Other in Your Money Life

The rigidity of some of the agreements couples make is amazing. So is the lack of respect and flexibility and the lack of commitment to the long-term health of the relationship. What is even more amazing, though, is the lack of trust two people often have for each other regarding money.

Think about it! You probably trust each other with the most precious parts of your life—your children. You see each other at your most vulnerable times—when you are ill, first thing in the morning, when you have been passed over at work and when you are grieving the loss of a loved one. You trust each other at these vulnerable times, yet you don't trust each other with money. Amazing! You trust each other with complete emotional and physical intimacy, yet you don't trust each other with money.

Money is a part of your long-term commitment to each other, so you need to turn this lack of trust around. In setting up a new way of working together with money, you must have the four cornerstones of your new money structure in place: commitment, respect, trust and compromise.

These cornerstones, anchored by your partnership values, will help you to begin sorting out responsibilities in your partnership. Maybe one of you needs to accept more responsibility for the big picture regarding your money—long-term retirement planning or your children's education, for example.

You aren't a child, and you need to share responsibility for these adult money decisions.

Maybe one of you needs to let go of control regarding money. You aren't the parent. You are sharing your life with a competent adult whom you trust in so many other ways, so now you need to learn to trust your partner regarding money, too. You need to let go of control and learn to trust yourself to compromise as you work together.

"Oh, right, Ruth," says Anne, with a bit of sarcasm in her voice. "If I didn't control the money and make sure we save enough, Neil would spend it all on toys. He may earn a great deal of money, but he can spend that and more if I let him."

Before Neil can respond, I tell them that the point of the work they are doing is to create a *system* that will "control" the money. Anne doesn't have to be controller. Neil doesn't have to feel controlled. Both of them agree to the rules of the money system, including how much to save and how much to spend on toys. The weekly money meetings are how you manage the system. So, as two competent, committed adults, you keep the rules of the system and, as you have been for six weeks, continue to hold weekly money meetings. That is what commitment is.

Creating a Money System Based on Trust

How much income do you each earn? You already calculated this in chapter 12, so just check back in your notes.

When you get your paycheck, your income from self-employment, or your investment income or child support, where is the check actually deposited? Into what account—yours, mine or ours?

The purpose of this book is to help you make your money life work in a way that also helps you form a stronger partnership. To do this, use the following model when depositing your income:

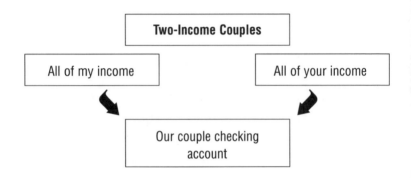

This diagram shows that all income, no matter what the source, is deposited into a couple checking account. This system blends the disparity of your incomes, and it is logistically more efficient. It is a symbol that in your partnership, you are both equally valued and you equally own the money. And as partners, you share equally the adult responsibility for making your money life work. Using this system, you will be able to practice commitment, respect, trust and compromise.

"Won't work!" David exclaims. "If I don't keep a handle on the money and keep some in my checkbook to take care of the bills when Julie overspends, we'll really go down the tube."

"We already *are* going down the tube," says Julie, "as you keep telling me. And besides, it's not my overspending you're worried about. You're worried you won't be able to hoard enough money in your checkbook for your precious hunting trip each fall."

Before David and Julie undo all the progress they have made, they need to see how easy it is to slip back into the old routine of blaming each other.

Just try this system of depositing your income into a couple checking account. If it doesn't work, you can always go back to the way you do it now. This book is about learning a *new* system. So try removing the control between the two of you and let the system provide the control.

Don't be afraid that the bills won't get paid. If you decide as partners to stay within the system, then the system will handle the bills. You have learned this with your cash system, right? Those weekly flexible expenses that used to be so variable are now quite predictable. The cash system of handling these flexible expenses is working. Remember how little you trusted each other six weeks ago when you began the weekly cash budget? Now look at you! As with the cash, you will feel a sense of control and predictability by using this system with the bigger budget you are evolving right now.

And, as individuals, you aren't left out of this system. The system has room for two individuals and a couple!

In the next diagram, you can see that out of your new couple checking account you will take out personal money. This personal money is called *autonomy money* and is for your expenses that are separate from your relationship. Autonomy money for each of you now becomes a bill that the couple checkbook pays to each of you—right up there next to your mortgage.

	Our Couple Checking Account	
My autonomy $		Your autonomy $

The question to ask yourself here is, "In our partnership, what expenses are *your* responsibilities, what are *my* responsibilities and what are *our* responsibilities? Use your cash budget as a starting place, but then you need to take this system one step further. You may want some of the bigger, annual expenses in your autonomy money, such as an annual hunting trip or retreat.

Some couples have very little money in their autonomy money—basically just what they need to get through the week, what I call *weekly running money*. Their other expenses are in their larger budget, which is managed at the weekly money meeting. Other couples cover everything that has anything to do with them separately in their autonomy money. Each pays for his or her car expenses, therapy, clothes or education. Most couples are somewhere in the middle of these two extremes.

Decide which expenses you want absolute control over. These are the expenses you don't want to have to justify to anyone. If you decide to not get your hair cut and instead spend more on clothes, that is your business. It is under your control. You can do whatever you want with this autonomy money as long as you can cover your expenses listed in the "Mine" section of the following chart.

Look back to the budget numbers you compiled in chapter 10. In your notebooks, draw sections that look like the following:

Monthly Expenses	Nonmonthly Expenses
Yours	
Haircut	Retreat: each August
Personal grooming items	
Newspapers/books	
$_____	$_____
Total	Total

Total = $_____

Monthly Expenses	Nonmonthly Expenses
Mine	
Personal grooming items	Haircut
Newspapers/books/	
tapes/flowers	
$_____	$_____
Total	Total

Total = $_____

Monthly Expenses	Nonmonthly Expenses
Ours	**Have-To**
Mortgage	Asset maintenance
Utilities	Medical/dental
Debt reduction (credit cards)	Home maintenance
	Home repair
	Car insurance/tags
	Life insurance
	Choice
	Vacation
	Major holidays
	Home furnishings
	Home fixings
$_____	$_____
Total	Total

Total = $_____

Use your budget numbers to fill in each section, listing the item and its cost. At this point, all you are doing is deciding *who*—you, your partner or the couple—is responsible for each expense. For example, the light bill for your home would be in the "Ours" section of the "Monthly Expenses." If you get your hair trimmed once a month or more frequently, it is probably in the "Mine" section of the "Monthly Expenses." If, on the other hand, you get your hair trimmed every six weeks, your hair would be under the "Mine" section of "Nonmonthly Expenses."

Don't simply organize your expenses according to what you are already doing. Think about your values and your partnership value statement. If you need your car to get to work to earn money to support your relationship, then maybe it would be fairer if the cost of maintaining that car was in the "Ours" section. There are no right or wrong answers here. But there are answers that will work better as you create your budget as partners.

Continue to fill in the chart until all items in your budget are represented. If you get discouraged, or if you start up an old fight or start blaming, stop!

Go back and read your partnership value statement. Go back and read your values. This material will help you remember why you are doing this and help you loosen up and try something new.

It's just money! You are simply organizing your money. Why would you hurt each other or your partnership? Come on! You've done harder things than this in your life. You are simply deciding what expense belongs to whom. That's all.

Now, add the totals for the sections labeled "Yours" and "Mine."

- How much money do *you* need to take care of both your monthly and nonmonthly expenses? This is the total of the two sections under "Mine."

- How much money does *your partner* need to take care of both monthly and nonmonthly expenses? This is the total of the two sections under "Yours."

Now, add the "Mine" and "Yours" sections to get figures for the "Ours" section:

- How much money is needed in the "Ours" section of "Monthly Expenses"?

- How much money is needed each month in the "Ours" section of "Nonmonthly Expenses" under the "Have-To" category?

- How much money is needed each month in the "Ours" section of "Nonmonthly Expenses" under the "Choice" category?

That's it! You're done with this chapter. You will use this information to actually set up a new budgeting system in chapter 14. Give yourself some credit for working through a very difficult chapter.

Before you go:

1. Set/confirm your next weekly money meeting. The agenda for this meeting follows this chapter.

2. Continue working with the cash. You're still learning.

3. Observe yourselves this week. See how often you compare yourself to your partner to see if your relationship is

really equal. Be aware of how frequently you feel resentment because you think your partner got the greater
share or the better deal.

4. Be aware when you feel angry or sad because you don't
   think your partner appreciates what you do—how much
   pressure you have at work, how hard you really do work,
   how carefully you shop or how exhausted you are. Be
   aware, and talk about it together, *without blame*. Use the
   four cornerstones—commitment, respect, trust and compromise—to help you have a discussion.

Money Meeting #7

Your seventh week of meeting—quite amazing, isn't it? You're almost done creating your new money system.

You have changed your money life in small steps—week after week. Of course, that is how all long-term change occurs. We live in a society that wants instant change—overnight success. But change that holds up over time occurs in small, consistent increments.

Remember when you first started your weekly money meetings how hard it was to find a time to meet? And now, even though your life is just as busy as it was seven weeks ago, you are finding the time. That's change.

Remember when you first started the weekly cash budget how this system was cumbersome and difficult? Remember how difficult it was to make the cash last all week or to remember to take cash with you when you went shopping? Now look at you! You have worked with cash for six weeks. That's change.

In the next chapter, you will continue this change. These changes may feel as cumbersome and difficult as the cash and the weekly money meetings once felt. But now you know that over time, you will feel more comfortable and the logistical problems will get easier. This knowledge will help you as you work through the next chapter.

Money Meeting Agenda

1. What did you observe about yourself this week? Did you find yourself feeling resentful as you compared yourself to your partner? Did you feel unappreciated at any time during the week? Were you able to talk about that feeling with your partner— and ask for some appreciation—without blaming? Take this time to talk together—with respect.

2. Go ahead and begin working through chapter 14.

Fourteen

Let's Do It!

You have established a solid foundation of values, and you have the four cornerstones of commitment, respect, trust and compromise in place to solidly anchor your new money structure. So, it's time to begin building your new money structure.

You have been learning and practicing for many weeks now, and you're ready for this next step. You have all the management tools, and you have compiled all the financial data you need to build this structure.

If you build your new money structure step by step, you won't feel so overwhelmed, and the structure will hold. Building your new money structure involves a set of decisions that you will make together. Many of these decisions involve detailed logistics. Each decision is essential in order to form a structure that works for you both.

Where Will You Keep Your Money?

On a clean sheet of paper in your notebooks, each of you should record the decisions you make—in case there's a question later. To make these decisions, you will need the information from chapter 13.

1. What checkbook will you use for the "Our" expenses category?

Do you already have a checkbook with both of your names printed on the checks? If so, get it and put a label on the outside of this checkbook that says either "Our Account" or "Joint Account." In this way you will physically name the account and while you're getting used to a new system you won't use the wrong checkbook.

If you don't have an account with both of your names on the checks, when will you open this account? What day? What time? At what bank?

This checkbook needs to stay at home with the bills. This way it is available to pay your bills at your weekly money meeting.

2. Will you continue with your weekly cash budget?

Please say yes. After all this work, it would be so easy to get sloppy and slip back into the old system. Weekly cash won't allow you to get sloppy or slip back. And because you are used to the weekly cash, it will be the familiar part of your new money structure.

If you will continue with cash, will you make any changes in the amount of cash or will you continue as is?

If you decide not to continue with cash, then you need to get a separate checkbook for your flexible living expenses. If you don't, these expenses will erode the money in your "Joint Account" checkbook. Remember how it used to be? Remember when you used to write all those small checks or go to the cash machine several times each week—and you couldn't figure out where all the money in the checkbook went? If you go back to that system and allow your weekly flexible living expenses to erode the money in the checkbook, they will also erode the trust you have built between you.

So, if you aren't going to use cash for these expenses, what checkbook will you use? Do you already have a checking account that could be used for these expenses? If you do, get that checkbook now and put a label on the outside that says "Weekly Flexible Expenses."

If you need to open a new account with both of your names on the checks, when will you do this? At what bank? When you open the new checking account, be sure to physically label the front of the checkbook as "Weekly Flexible Expenses."

Decide, together, where you will physically keep this checkbook. Will one of you be responsible for the spending that comes out of this checkbook? Or will you keep it in a specific place so either of you can take it when needed? There is no right answer here. Just be clear about your decision.

3. Where will your autonomy money be kept?

Each of you needs to make that decision. Do you want to keep it in cash, in a checkbook, in a savings account or in some combination of those three? Again, there is no right answer here. You just have to decide.

You both don't have to handle your autonomy money in the same way. You get to decide what works best for you. You will be receiving your autonomy money from the "Joint Account" in the form of a check, so you need to know what you are physically going to do with that money.

4. Do you have a savings account at the same bank as the "Joint Account" to hold your "Nonmonthly Have-To" expenses?

The most efficient way to hold the money you will need for "Nonmonthly Have-To" expenses is in a savings account at the same bank as the "Joint Account" checkbook. You want to be able to transfer money between these two accounts by telephone.

If you have such a savings account, are both your names and Social Security numbers listed on the bank records? If not, add them.

If you don't have this type of savings account at the same bank as the "Joint Account," when can you open one?

Decide where you will keep the statements for this savings account. A file folder with sides, so nothing slips out, works best. Mark this folder "Our Nonmonthly Have-To Account."

5. Where will you keep your "Nonmonthly Choice" money?

You can keep this money in cash, in a checking account or in a savings account. If you will need this money to buy clothes for the children or furnishings for the house, you may want to have this money in cash or in a checking account so you have ready access to it. You can keep some of the "Nonmonthly Choice" money in envelopes for awhile. Until you've had more time to make progress in your money life, you may not have enough to open another savings or checking account. Then cash in envelopes works best.

You may decide that having money in envelopes helps you make decisions together, without any hard feelings such as, "You bought a new what? I was going to use that money for something else for our family."

Just decide what you believe will work best logistically and will keep you within your budget so you can keep building trust between you.

You can always change this decision if as you go along you find it isn't working as well as it could.

You are doing well so far. Let's keep going.

How Do We Actually Get Started?

1. How will our net income get into our "Joint Account"?

Who is responsible for depositing paychecks, child support, investment income or any other income? Write down what *you* agree to do so you don't forget.

2. If you are using cash for your weekly flexible expenses, who will get the cash?

You or me? On what day each week? How much cash will be withdrawn from the bank each week?

If you are not using cash for your weekly flexible expenses, who will deposit the money in the appropriate checking account? On what day or date? How much money will be deposited?

Write down these agreements.

3. **Who will transfer money from the "Joint Account" to the "Nonmonthly Have-To Account"?**

   Most couples decide that the task of transferring money into and out of this account can be done at their weekly money meetings. If you want to do this, write it down.

   If you have any ideas that you think will work better for you, as a couple, write them down.

4. **Who will deposit money into the "Nonmonthly Choice Account"? Or, who will take the money out in cash for these expenses?**

   Just make a decision.

5. **How will you receive your autonomy money?**

   Your autonomy money is a "Monthly Have-To" expense. What works best for most couples is to pay yourselves once a month. Most couples choose to write these checks as one of their tasks in the weekly money meeting.

   Write down your decision.

   What you do with the check once you get it is your personal business. But don't forget, if you run out of money, there is no place within the budget for you to "dip." Plan this money carefully so you can take care of your personal needs and wants.

Organizing the Budget Itself

When do you receive your monthly income—salaried or self-employed income, investment income, rental income or child support? On what day or date each month? Make a list of all income with the date that you receive it:

Type of Income	Date Income Is Received
1. _____	_____
2. _____	_____
3. _____	_____
4. _____	_____

What money will you have available by the *fourth week* of the month to pay your *first*-of-the-month bills? We'll call this amount of money "Bill-Paying A." Write down the amount of income that's available for the first-of-the-month bills.

What money will you have available by the *second week* of the month to pay the *middle*-of-the-month bills? We'll call this amount of money "Bill-Paying B." Write down the amount of income that's available for the middle-of-the-month bills:

Bill-Paying A	Bill-Paying B
Amount of income	Amount of income
$_____	$_____

Now, look at the diagram you made in chapter 13 called "Yours, Mine or Ours." In the "Ours" section of the "Monthly Expenses" column of this diagram, you listed the specific expenses and their costs. Write down the due date for each monthly expense if it has one. For example, your mortgage is probably due on the first of the month, so the mortgage will be written in the "Bill-Paying A" column. Your electric bill may be due on the twentieth of the month, so the electric bill will be written in the "Bill-Paying B" column.

We are still working with just the "Monthly Expenses." Make two lists, based on the due date of each bill:

Bill-Paying A	Bill-Paying B
1. Mortgage $_____	1. Electric $_____
2. $_____	2. $_____
3. $_____	3. $_____
4. $_____	4. $_____
Total $_____	Total $_____

What is the total amount of income you have for each time period—each column? Check your calculations.

Subtract the amount of expense in each column from the amount of income available for each column:

Bill-Paying A	Bill-Paying B
Total income $_____	Total income $_____
−	−
Total bills $_____	Total bills $_____
=	=
The amount of income available for remaining expenses	The amount of income available for remaining expenses
$_____	$_____

Using the income that is remaining for each bill-paying column, start to make decisions about when your other expenses will be paid. These are the expenses that need to be paid but don't have a specific due date, so you can pay them in either column. For example, when will you each get your autonomy money? Or, how much in each time period will you transfer to the "Nonmonthly Have-To" savings account?

Keep working until all expenses are on one of the lists *and* you haven't spent more than the amount of income available for that time period.

When you start to get discouraged, think of this as a two-thousand-piece jigsaw puzzle. The pieces will fit. It just takes time.

You have to do this part or all the work you have accomplished so far won't change anything. You have to keep working together. If you quit, you won't know when to pay what. You will be confused, and then it's easy to blame each other. The thought of this happening should make you more determined than ever to make this work. If you need a break, take one and then come back and finish.

You're working on the logistics—the details—and they need to be in order and clear. You are planning so your money life is clear and in order. There isn't a quick way through this step. So just keep working.

When you get everything to fit, shake each other's hands. Congratulations!

Weekly Money Meetings

Once you're finished working through this book, you will need to have an ongoing agenda for your weekly money meetings. I recommend that you number the four weeks of the month on your calendar—one, two, three and four. Now that was easy. These numbers correspond to the four money meeting agendas that follow. The number on your calendar will tell you which agenda to follow when you sit down for a money meeting.

Money Meeting Agenda—Week #1

1. Set/confirm when you will meet next week for your meeting.

2. Put the cash for your weekly cash budget into the envelopes. You have already decided who will get the cash.

3. Go through the expenditures for both the "Nonmonthly Have-To" expenses and the "Nonmonthly Choice" expenses. Look ahead to any expenses coming up. Will there be enough money to cover those expenses? This is simply a planning time for the nonmonthly expenses.

4. Review your goal time-frame sheet from chapter 9. What do you need to do this month to stay on track with the time frame of your goals? What will each of you do by the next money meeting?

5. Make a commitment.

Money Meeting Agenda—Week #2

1. Set/confirm when you will meet next week for your meeting.

2. Put the cash for your weekly cash budget into the envelopes. You have already decided who will get the cash.

3. This is "Bill-Paying B" week. Pay any bills listed in the "Bill-Paying B" column during the meeting. Actually write out the bills and get them ready to mail.

4. If you are supposed to *deposit* money into your "Non-monthly Have-To Account," who will make the telephone transfer? If you are supposed to *deposit* money into your "Nonmonthly Choice Account," you have to either deposit money into that account or get the cash, depending on how you have decided to handle this money. Who will take care of this task? If you need to *pay* a nonmonthly have-to bill, who will call and transfer the money from the savings account?

Money Meeting Agenda—Week #3

1. Set/confirm when you will meet next week for your meeting.

2. Put the cash for your weekly cash budget into the envelopes. You have already decided who will get the cash.

3. This is a good week to reconcile your checkbooks. Work together to make sure your bank statements and the balances in your checkbook registers match. One of you can read through the checks aloud, while the other marks them off in the register. If neither of you knows how to do this, if neither of you is willing to do this task or if you are unable to reconcile your accounts with the bank's statements, take your checkbook(s) into the bank and ask for help. You need to be sure you are working with an accurate balance or you may overdraft an account.

Overdraft fees are not in your budget! Decide who will take the information to the bank and when.

Money Meeting Agenda—Week #4

1. Set/confirm when you will meet next week for your meeting.

2. Put the cash for your weekly cash budget into the envelopes. You have already decided who will get the cash.

3. This week is "Bill-Paying A" week. Pay any bills listed in the "Bill-Paying A" column during the meeting. Get the work done so the bills are ready for mailing.

Exercise: Committing to Your Next Weekly Money Meeting

1. Before you complete this chapter, decide the day, time and place of your next weekly money meeting.

2. Which week number in this month is next week— one, two, three or four? Make sure you both know which agenda you will use at the next meeting. Your next meeting, just like every weekly money meeting, is the structural anchor to your money life. If you meet weekly, you can solve any money problem before it gets too large. The weekly meetings allow you to resolve any blame or frustration between you and your partner before those feelings become unmanageable. Using the four money meeting agendas outlined in this chapter will make your money life

---

quite manageable. Just think, you now know you can manage your new money structure in *less* than one hour each week!

3. Take just a moment now to renew your commitment to each other that you will continue to meet—week after week after week.

Rules for Your New Money Structure

There are just three rules you and your partner must follow if you want your new money structure to hold over the long term:

1. NO withdrawing money from any of your joint accounts without discussing the withdrawal with your partner.

This rule shows that you respect your partner. It will help you continue to build trust—neither of you will be able to "surprise" the other. Most of your expenditures can be discussed at your weekly meetings, so there should be no need to withdraw money between meetings.

This rule holds except for an emergency. An emergency is *not* a sale on clothes or computers. An emergency is an unexpected medical need or when the car is stalled on the freeway and needs to be towed.

2. If you don't have the money to pay for something, you don't spend the money.

This rule, before the age of revolving credit card balances, was obvious to most people. Now, this needs to be a rule if you and your partner are going to continue to build a healthy money life and build trust.

This rule means that if you or your partner finds a really good deal on airline tickets, and you have been wanting to get away, you will get the tickets *only* if you have the money accumulated in your "Nonmonthly Choice Account." If you don't have the money, you don't get the tickets. You will need to be creative: How can you get away and not break the structure—the rules of your new money life? Brainstorm!

Also remember that no matter how good the sale— whether on airline tickets, clothes, computers, cars or furniture—there will always be another sale, maybe even better than this one. Start to trust that thought, and save your money for the next and better sale.

3. **If your weekly cash budget runs out and you can't delay spending money until your next cash payday, you must take the money you need out of your "Nonmonthly Choice Account."**

Of course, you only do this after you have talked to your partner, so you don't erode the trust you are building between you.

This rule means that the extra cash you need to get through the week needs to come from your vacation money, holiday money, children's clothing money, home furnishings money or any of your other "Nonmonthly Choice" categories. Be careful, though, because when the next holiday comes or the next sale to end all sales on the couch you have been eyeing for your living room happens, you're going to be disappointed if you've already spent the money.

Make the commitment to each other that you will follow these three rules. If you do this, your new money structure will work and you will continue to build trust between you.

How Will You Know if the Money System Is Working?

- **You will know the system is working if you are meeting weekly.**

    If you miss a meeting, don't rationalize *why* you missed it—you didn't feel well, your child didn't feel well, the in-laws visited, the dog had puppies, you got caught at the office. Instead of rationalizing, ask yourselves why you *really* missed the meeting. If it really was impossible to meet, why didn't you reschedule? If you had to miss a key meeting at work, you would reschedule, right? The weekly money meeting is a key meeting. If it's impossible to make it, respectfully reschedule the meeting with your partner.

    If missing or rescheduling meetings becomes a habit, go back over chapter 5 and figure out what belief is keeping you from honoring your commitment. Then renew your commitment to meet weekly.

- **You will know the system is working if all bills are paid *on time,* including the nonmonthly bills.**

    If your monthly bills are paid on time, then your system of using "Bill-Paying A" and "Bill-Paying B" categories is working. If the monthly bills are sometimes paid late, work with those items. Even if, for now, you are paying only minimum payments, make sure the bills are paid on time. When you do this, you are building trust with your partner and your creditors.

Be patient as you wait for the "Nonmonthly Have-To Account" to get funded enough to pay all the non-monthly bills on time. It will take several months before you *know* the money will be in the savings account when it's time to pay the car insurance or a car repair bill or the house taxes. The system just needs time to accumulate money in this account. Creatively juggle until that happens and be patient.

- **You will know the system is working when you're meeting the goals that you set for yourselves.**

   You have already made a commitment to evaluate your goals each month as part of the "Money Meeting Agenda—Week #1." If you are making progress toward your goals, the system is working.

   If one of your goals is to reduce debt—is the debt going down?

   If one of your goals is to retire early, have you increased the money you put into retirement funds?

   If one of your goals is to travel to Tibet, are you learning about Tibet and saving money towards that trip?

   If one of your goals is to start your own business, are you taking seminars, reading books and saving money for the start-up time?

   Keep track of where you are with your goals. If you're getting closer to them, you know the system is working.

- **You will know the system is working if your money life feels fair to both of you.**

   As long-term partners, this is probably the most important measure of the system's success. Your money structure may be working wonderfully, but, as you have already learned, if it doesn't feel fair, it won't work in the long term. If resentment in either of you is building, talk about it. Don't resist the information from your partner that he or she feels resentful. Be willing to talk about what is causing the resentment. Be willing to listen and creatively solve the problem.

Remember, this new money system will work if the budget numbers balance *and* the decisions you make feel fair to both of you. Success is as simple as that.

Epilogue

Y ou're on your own now. If you get stuck, work through this book again. Or use the book as a reference—go back to the chapter that can help you with a particular problem.

If you are still stuck, you may need a different kind of help. Several of the couples you heard from in this book needed to sit down with a marriage therapist and work through blame, shame, anger and resentment. You also might need a professional to help you work through your "stuck places." If you need help, please get it! By all means, don't lose heart. Don't give up on each other or on your long-term commitment. Your relationship is a priceless investment. Protect it!

You have worked so hard to learn to work together in your money life. Look at all you now know about yourselves and each other. You are both quite remarkable, aren't you?

Remember, when you are angry or hurt because of a money decision your partner made—and you want to say something mean or sarcastic—*be nice!* Speak respectfully. This is your lifetime partner. You don't want to lose each other. Remember, it's just money, for goodness' sake!

Index

239